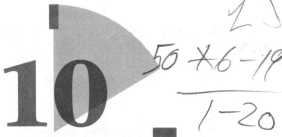

10

MINUTE GUIDE TO

401(K) PLANS

By Paul Katzeff

Macmillan Spectrum/Alpha

A Division of Macmillan Publishing
A Simon & Schuster Macmillan Company
1633 Broadway, New York, NY 10019

International Standard Book Number: 0-02-861117-9
Library of Congress Card Catalog Number: 96-068552

98 97 96   8 7 6 5 4 3 2 1

Interpretation of the printing code: the rightmost double-digit number is the year of the book's first printing; the rightmost single-digit number is the number of the book's printing. For example, a printing code of 96-1 shows that this copy of the book was printed during the first printing of the book in 1996.

Printed in the United States of America

Reasonable care has been taken in the preparation of the text to ensure its clarity and accuracy. This book is sold with the understanding that the author and the publisher are not engaged in rendering legal, accounting, or other professional service. Laws vary from state to state, and readers with specific financial questions should seek the services of a professional advisor.

The author and publisher specifically disclaim any liability, loss, or risk, personal or otherwise, which is incurred as a consequence, directly or indirectly, of the use and application of any of the contents of this book.

Publisher Theresa Murtha
Managing Editor Michael Cunningham
Development Editor Debra Wishik Englander
Production Editor Phil Kitchel
Cover Designer Dan Armstrong
Designer Kim Scott
Production Supervisor Laurie Casey
Indexer Chris Wilcox
Production Team Heather Butler, Angela Calvert, Dan Caparo, Krena Lanham, Christine Tyner, Megan Wade, Christy Wagner

CONTENTS

1 INTRODUCING 401(K) PLANS   **1**
What Is a 401(k) Plan? 1
What a 401(k) Plan Does 2

2 ADVANTAGES OF 401(K) PLANS   **5**
Other Advantages of 401(k) Plans 6
Tax-Deferred Dollars 6

3 DETERMINING YOUR ELIGIBILITY   **10**
Eligibility for Enrollment 10

4 UNDERSTANDING YOUR COMPANY'S PLAN   **12**
Getting Started 12
The Key Sources of Information 13

5 WITHDRAWING YOUR MONEY   **17**
Knowing When You Are Eligible To Take Money Out 17
The Proper Way To Take Out Money 19

6 CALCULATING HOW MUCH TO SAVE   **25**

7 UNDERSTANDING RISK   **36**
What Do They Mean, Anyway? 37
Applying This to Your 401(k) Plan 38
The Numbers Game 40

8 COPING WITH RISK: FIRST TACTIC   **41**

9 COPING WITH RISK: SECOND TACTIC   **44**

10 COPING WITH RISK: THIRD TACTIC   **50**
Focusing In 51
Recovery May Be Swift 52

11 FIND OUT YOUR RISK TOLERANCE   **55**
Seek the Correct Balance 55
Your Risk Tolerance Will Change 56

12 ASSET ALLOCATION   **62**
Finding the Right Fit 69

13 SELECTING INVESTMENTS   **75**
Seven Guidelines 75

14 Understanding Your Own 401(k) Plan Account   **79**
First, Understand the National Ground Rules 79
Two Sets of Rules 80
Next, Learn Your Company's Rules 82
Outside Sources of Information 86
Specializing in Mutual Funds 87

15 Judging Mutual Fund Performance   **88**
How To Use Total Return 89

16 Your Mutual Fund Expenses   **92**
Costs Vary Among Funds 93
A Variety of Fees and Expenses 93

17 Contributing to Your Account   **97**
How Much Are You Allowed To Contribute to
  Your Account? 97
Two Other Restrictions 99

18 Additional Contributions to Your Account   **102**
A Key Benefit of 401(k) Plans 102
After-Tax Contributions 106

19 Vesting   **108**
When You Become Vested 109
How Vesting Helps You 110
Other Considerations 114

20 Borrowing Money from Your Account   **115**
What Is the Loan Feature and How Does It Work? 115
The Pros and Cons of Borrowing 120

21 Hardship Distribution   **122**
The Key Differences 122
How To Qualify for a Hardship Withdrawal 123

22 Coping with Life's Emergencies   **125**
Divorce or Family Support 125
In the Event of Your Death 126
If Your Plan Ends..128

23 Safeguarding Your Account   **129**
Ten Warning Signs 129

Index   **133**

Introduction

Saving and investing for retirement is one of the most significant decisions you'll have to make. 401(k) plans are one of the best tools you can use to build your retirement nest egg.

But if you plot the wrong strategy—by planning either too aggressively or too conservatively—you could cost yourself hundreds of thousands of dollars. If uncertainty makes you afraid to make any plans at all, you will lose even more. In fact, fully 25 percent of the workers eligible to participate in a 401(k) plan don't even take advantage of this opportunity.* Planning properly, though, is not difficult, especially if you have easy-to-understand guidance. That's what this book, the *10 Minute Guide to 401(k) Plans*, provides.

This book will help you decide how much money you'll need at retirement, and how much you should save and invest to build that nest egg. It will also teach you how a 401(k) plan makes your money grow, and how to use a 401(k) to reach your retirement goals. It will even translate into plain English the ins and outs of saving and investing, and make investment decisions simple and easy.

Think of the *10 Minute Guide to 401(k) Plans* as a supplement to the information you receive from your employer. You may work in some far-flung outpost of a large corporation and not receive adequate details about your company plan. Even if you're lucky enough to work for a company that tries to provide helpful information, the information may be confusing.

Obviously, you'll need more than 10 minutes to plan your retirement. This guide will break your planning process into easy-to-follow 10-minute lessons. It will explain how you can use a 401(k) plan to accumulate money for your retirement. This book will help you make the most of your 401(k) plan—whether you just became eligible, or you've been postponing enrollment in your company's plan, or even if you've been contributing to your plan for years.

Why the 10 Minute Guide to 401(k) Plans?

The *10 Minute Guide to 401(k) Plans* presents a series of steps that you can take to make the most of this retirement plan. Each lesson introduces important subjects and it takes you about 10 minutes to gain the basics of each lesson. By the time you complete the book, you will have gained a working knowledge of how to maximize your 401(k) plan account. While you may want to jump ahead to a particular subject, you should start at Lesson 1 and work your way through the book, because the book is organized to explain information and provide retirement strategies in a logical progression.

Conventions Used in This Book

To help you move through the lessons easily, the *10 Minute Guide to 401(k) Plans* uses the following icons to identify useful facts:

 Plain English   New or unfamiliar terms are defined in (you got it) "plain English."

 Timesaver Tip   These are ideas that will help you avoid confusion.

 Panic Button   This icon is used to highlight problems that readers often have and offers simple solutions.

How To Start Making the Most of Your 401(k) Plan

There's no reason why you shouldn't take full advantage of your 401(k). All you need is to enroll and simple instructions on how to get the most from your plan. In this book, you will learn how a 401(k) plan works, how to choose investments that are right for you, and how to avoid problems while you build your retirement nest egg.

The *10 Minute Guide to 401(k) Plans* puts you in charge of one of the most important parts of your life.

Acknowledgments

*Source: Access Research, Inc., Windsor, CT; reprinted with permission.

Special thanks to David England of Waddell & Reed and Harry Kluger of Lexington Savings Bank for their contributions to this book, and to my editor, Debra Wishik Englander, for her encouragement and vision.

INTRODUCING
401(K) PLANS

In this lesson, you will learn what a 401(k) plan is and its advantages.

WHAT IS A 401(K) PLAN?

Whether you're facing retirement in the next few years or have just entered the workforce, you can no longer count on Social Security or traditional pension plans to provide enough money for your retirement. Fortunately, though, there is another retirement plan that offers many advantages to employees: the 401(k) plan.

 401(k) The name is taken from the section of the Internal Revenue code that spells out what these retirement plans are. The government calls them a *cash or deferred arrangement* (CODA) retirement plan. But everyone else simply uses the nickname 401(k).

In the jargon of pension planning, a 401(k) plan is called a *defined-contribution* plan.

Defined-contribution plan This term refers to a pension plan like a 401(k), which requires that specific amounts (in dollars or percentage of pay) are contributed but does not specify how much an employee will receive as a retirement benefit. This type of plan differs from traditional pension plans, *defined benefits plans*, which promise to pay employees specific amounts of money after they retire.

401(k) plans have become popular because they:

- Reduce current taxes on your salary.

- Let you invest money without paying current taxes on it or the money it earns.

- Offer an alternative source of retirement income. This is particularly important since you may not be certain how much savings, Social Security, or traditional pension-plan income you'll have when you retire.

WHAT A 401(K) PLAN DOES

A 401(k) plan enables you to build a better nest egg than anything you can do on your own:

- First, your 401(k) money is tax-deductible—or, in IRS lingo, it is *before-tax* money. This means you get to sock away the cash *before* it is counted as part of your taxable income. This reduces your tax bill. For example, if you're in the 28 percent tax bracket, you save 28 cents in taxes on every dollar you contribute to your plan. That's the same as a guaranteed 28 percent interest or return. *And that's before you even put the money to work in an investment, earning more money!* Compare that to the meager 4 or 5 percent interest your bank account is probably earning.

- Second, this tax-deferred money grows. By investing it, you put these savings to work, earning you more money—also tax-free, until the day you retire, possibly decades from now.

- Third, your employer may make a *matching* contribution to your 401(k) account, approaching or equalling what you put in. Most employers will match your contributions, up to a limit, by 50 percent. If your employer contributes 50 cents for every dollar you do, that's an extra 50 percent return each year you get that match. Again, this is even before you put the money to work.

Those are some of the key reasons why 401(k) plans are growing in popularity, attracting about 2 million new participants each year.

- There are now 22 million Americans enrolled in 401(k) plans, more than double the number of participants in 1985.

- 401(k) plans now hold $675 billion retirement dollars, more than six-fold the amount they controlled in 1985.

- 228,000 companies now offer 401(k) plans to their employees, more than triple the number of sponsors in 1985.

With workers and businesses increasingly reliant on them, it is growing more important to understand the benefits a 401(k) plan offers you and how you can take the fullest advantage of them.

In this lesson, you have learned what a 401(k) plan is. In the next lesson, you will learn how to make the most of the advantages your 401(k) plan offers.

ACKNOWLEDGMENTS

Source of data concerning employee participation and growth of 401(k) plans: Access Research, Inc., Windsor, CT; reprinted with permission.

ADVANTAGES OF 401(K) PLANS

In this lesson, you will learn the advantages of a 401(k) plan.

A 401(k) plan lets your money grow through investments. You invest a fraction of your current pay so that it grows into a large retirement kitty.

Of all pension plans, a 401(k) gives you the most control over your money. It gives you the power to make your money grow faster or slower, a flexibility other pension plans don't usually offer you.

Here's what happens:

- You select a dollar amount or percentage of your pay to contribute.

- You're almost always offered a choice of investments.

- You're permitted to change the amount you contribute periodically. Ditto for your selection of investments.

- You're free to invest aggressively and seek higher rates of return, or growth, for your money. Or you can choose a safer but less rewarding course. Historically, the higher your risk, the greater your payoff.

- You don't worry about having to play stockbroker. Although choosing investments is often up to you, you don't have to manage the investments themselves. The investments are frequently mutual funds, which typically own shares in other companies' stock. All you have to do is choose which mutual funds you want.

OTHER ADVANTAGES OF 401(K) PLANS

401(k) plans offer additional benefits:

- Most plans let you borrow your own money at rates frequently a lot lower than interest rates on credit cards.

- You may be allowed to make after-tax contributions. Although you pay taxes on the money like any earned income, once you stash it away into an after-tax 401(k) account its earnings do escape current taxes.

- You *can* take it with you! If you leave your current workplace, your 401(k) account is as much yours as that family photo on your desk. You are generally free to reinvest it in the 401(k) at your new workplace or another tax-deferred account like an Individual Retirement Account (IRA).

TAX-DEFERRED DOLLARS

Your 401(k) money is tax-deductible, which means it is not counted as part of your taxable income except for your Social Security and Medicare calculation. It also grows without taxes eating away at it. This is a tremendous advantage!

Let's say you're a single taxpayer, earning $40,000, and in the 28 percent tax bracket. Table 2.1 illustrates your various choices.

- Column 1 shows what happens if you participate in a 401(k) plan and contribute $2,000 a year. The tax bite from your paycheck is reduced, and your investment income is protected from taxes (until you retire).

- Column 2 shows what happens if you don't invest in a 401(k).

- Column 3 shows how an investment in your 401(k) plan earns more than your same investment outside of the 401(k) plan because your 401(k) investment income is not taxable, but your outside investment's income is.

tip

In addition to accumulating on a tax-deferred basis, your 401(k) investments offer the added benefit of compounding. Each year, your investment grows by the amount you contribute plus the interest from the previous year. Compounding is like a turbo-booster on your investments.

The advantage of tax-deferred money is that you get to keep the money that you lose otherwise to the tax collector. This table shows how your income is greater with a 401(k) plan than without, even when you make the same investment outside the tax-protection of a 401(k) plan. (The table makes the hypothetical assumption that your investment earns 9 percent a year.)

TABLE 2.1   GAINING AN EDGE

WITH A 401(K)	WITHOUT A 401(K) OR AN INVESTMENT	WITHOUT A 401(K) BUT WITH AN INVESTMENT
Gross income = $40,000	Gross income = $40,000	Gross income = $40,000
Contribution: $2,000; reduces gross income for tax purposes to $38,000	Contribution: None; gross income for tax purposes remains $40,000	Contribution: $2,000, but without 401(k), taxable income isn't reduced; gross income for tax purposes remains $40,000

continues

TABLE 2.1   CONTINUED

WITH A 401(K)	WITHOUT A 401(K) OR AN INVESTMENT	WITHOUT A 401(K) BUT WITH AN INVESTMENT
Standard deduction & personal exemption excludes first $6,400 from taxes	Standard deduction & personal exemption excludes first $6,400 from taxes	Standard deduction & personal exemption excludes first $6,400 from taxes
Tax on $6,400 to $29,750 of income at 15% rate = $3,503	Tax on $6,400 to $29,750 of income at 15% rate = $3,503	Tax on $6,400 to $29,750 of income at 15% rate = $3,503
Tax remaining: $8,250 × 28% $2,310	Tax remaining: $10,250 × 28% $2,870	Tax remaining: $10,250 × 28% $2,870
Net income: $38,000 – $5,813 $32,187	Net income: $40,000 – $6,373 $33,627	Net income: $40,000 – $6,373 $33,627
Meanwhile, $2,000 contribution grows at 9% = $180	N.A.	Meanwhile, $2,000 contribution grows at 9% = $180
Tax on $180: None; this is tax-deferred income	N.A.	Tax: $180 × 28% $50.40
Adjusted net income: $32,187 + $180 $32,367	Adjusted net income: $33,627	Adjusted net income: $33,627 + $129.60 ($180-$50.40) $33,756.60
Still have $2,000, so amount you control after first year: $32,367 + $2,000 $34,367	N.A. (The $2,000 is part of the $40,000 gross.)	N.A. (The $2,000 is part of the $40,000 gross.)
Your bottom line: **$34,367**	Your bottom line: **$33,627**	Your bottom line: **$33,757**

Source: Dave England, Waddell & Reed

So, one of the basic features of 401(k) plans—their double tax break—puts more money in your possession—either as take-home pay or as dollars and cents in your 401(k) plan account. And it does it every year you participate.

In this lesson, you learned what the features of a 401(k) plan are, and how they can work to your advantage. In the next lesson, you will learn whether you can join your workplace's 401(k) and if so, when.

ACKNOWLEDGMENTS

Input to analysis: financial planner Dee Lee, Harvard Financial Educators, Harvard, Mass.

DETERMINING YOUR ELIGIBILITY

In this lesson, you will learn whether you are eligible to enroll in your workplace's 401(k) plan and, if so, how soon.

ELIGIBILITY FOR ENROLLMENT

The federal government allows an employer to restrict you from participating in your workplace's 401(k) plan, but the restrictions are usually no big deal.

The most important eligibility standards are simple:

- Your employer is allowed to prohibit you from joining until you've worked up to a full year for the business.

- Your employer is also allowed to prohibit you from joining until you're 21 years old.

Time Is Money   You can get credit for a year's service in less than a year. Here's how: Your employer is permitted to calculate your eligibility period either by counting the number of months you work or the number of hours you work. If your employer uses the hours method, he must credit you for a full year once you work at least 1,000 hours in a 12-month period, even if it took you less than 12 months.

Equal Credit   If you transfer from one part of a company that does not offer a 401(k) into another that does, your employer has to credit you for all of your time of service with the company in calculating your eligibility for participation (and for "vesting"—something you'll learn more about in Lesson 20).

Your employer is allowed to make other restrictions as well:

- Your employer does not have to offer a 401(k) plan to all employees. If your employer is a large, diversified corporation, for example, only employees in certain divisions may be eligible. Perhaps only unionized workers will be eligible. Maybe only hourly workers, or only salaried.

Your Plan Administrator or personnel or human resources department can tell you what the eligibility requirements are for your company's plan.

Who's in charge?   Don't be surprised if your personnel or human resources manager knows less about the 401(k) plan than you do. Nobody's perfect. The Plan Administrator is ultimately responsible for answering your questions.

ACKNOWLEDGMENTS

Input regarding enrollment eligibility: Robert Liberto and Frank Picarelli, The Segal Co., New York; and David Godofsky, Bryan, Pendleton, Swats & McAllister, Nashville, Tenn.

4

UNDERSTANDING YOUR COMPANY'S PLAN

In this lesson, you will learn the basics of how your 401(k) plan works.

GETTING STARTED

It may help to compare your 401(k) plan to a baseball team. There are a variety of people involved in keeping the team playing, from the owner, manager, scouts, and coaches to the players—like you. Your 401(k) plan also has a specific organization with different people responsible for various jobs. Here are the rules and the people you should familiarize yourself with:

Sponsor Your employer, who offers you the plan, is known as the *sponsor*. Your employer has the final word on decisions such as which investment options the plan will have. Your employer also hires, designates, or approves all the other key personnel.

Trustee The individual, group, or committee that has overall responsibility. The trustee reports to the sponsor.

Plan administrator   The person who provides you with information, although he or she may do that through the personnel or human resources department.

Investment manager   Usually an outside firm that buys and sells your investments for you.

Recordkeeper   Generally an outside firm that keeps track of such things as how much you contribute. For a large plan, the recordkeeper and investment manager are likely to be separate companies. Sometimes, though, the same firm provides both services.

THE KEY SOURCES OF INFORMATION

Besides knowing who is responsible for running your plan, you also need to know how much you can contribute, when you will be *vested*, whether you can borrow from your plan, how much your employer will contribute, and so on. You'll read about these features in later lessons.

This important information is found in three documents that your employer is required to provide. Each document contains specific data about your 401(k) plan.

Summary plan description   The SPD tells you what your company plan provides and how it operates. It explains such things as when you can start participating in the plan, how your service and benefits are calculated, when you become vested, and when you will receive payment. Also, it explains how you can file a claim for benefits, under what circumstances you can lose your benefits, and how to file an appeal. It also has the name and address of your plan administrator.

Summary annual report   The SAR summarizes the financial reports that most plans file with the U.S. Department of Labor. For more details about your plan's assets, ask your plan administrator for a copy of the plan's complete annual report.

Individual benefit statement   The document that describes your total accrued and vested benefits. It is a summary of what is in your account.

There is another useful document that you can get:

Summary of material modifications   This summarizes any changes to your company's plan. If the plan is changed, you must be given a copy of this or a revised SPD.

Table 4.1 summarizes how and when you can get a copy of each of these documents and whether there is any cost.

TABLE 4.1   SOURCES OF PLAN INFORMATION

DOCUMENT	FROM WHOM YOU CAN GET IT	WHEN YOU CAN GET IT	YOUR COST
Summary plan description	Plan administrator	Automatically within 90 days of your enrollment in the plan	Free
		Automatically every 5 years if your plan is amended	Free
		Automatically every 10 years if your plan has not been amended	Free
		Within 30 days of your request	Reasonable charge

DOCUMENT	FROM WHOM YOU CAN GET IT	WHEN YOU CAN GET IT	YOUR COST
	U.S. Dept. of Labor	Upon request	Copying charge
Summary annual report	Plan administrator	Automatically 9 months after the end of plan year (which may be its fiscal year for accounting purposes), or 2 months after the filing of the annual report.	Free
	U.S. Dept. of Labor	Upon request	Copying charge
Annual report	Plan administrator	Within 30 days of a written request	Reasonable charge
	U.S. Dept. of Labor	Upon request	Copying charge
Individual benefit statement	Plan administrator	Once every 12 months	Free
Summary of material modifica-tions	Plan administrator	Automatically within 210 days after the end of the plan year for which the plan has been amended	Free
	U.S. Dept. of Labor	Upon request	Copying charge

Source: U.S. Dept. of Labor

There are also other ways you can get information about your plan.

THE WRITTEN WORD

It may take only a simple oral request to get a document from your employer. But if a document is not readily available, make your request in writing, especially if you work for a large corporation or your plan administrator works in a another city. This way, you'll have a record of your request, triggering the plan administrator's responsibility under federal law to reply.

Federal Assistance   You may also get a summary plan description, summary annual report, or annual report by writing to the U.S. Dept. of Labor, PWBA, Public Disclosure Room, Room N-5638, 200 Constitution Ave., NW, Washington, DC, 20210.

Your chances of getting a quick and accurate response are improved if you specify the name of the plan, your company's employer identification number (a 9-digit number assigned by the IRS, which you can get from the plan administrator, personnel or human resources dept.), and the plan number (a 3-digit number).

Remember, not only should you learn about your individual account but you should understand how your company plan operates generally.

In this lesson, you learned how a 401(k) plan works. In the next lesson, you'll learn when you can start to withdraw money from your plan.

WITHDRAWING YOUR MONEY

In this lesson, you will learn when you can start to withdraw your money from your 401(k) plan and what the penalties are for early withdrawal.

KNOWING WHEN YOU ARE ELIGIBLE TO TAKE MONEY OUT

If you withdraw money from your 401(k) plan account before you are eligible, you will have to pay hefty penalties. You become eligible to withdraw money under these circumstances:

- You reach age 59 ¹/₂.

- You die or become totally and permanently disabled.

- You incur deductible medical expenses, which exceed 7.5 percent of your adjusted gross income.

- You were at least 55 years old when you quit your job or were fired, laid off, or took formal early retirement.

- You arrange a schedule of annuitized *distributions* (roughly equal, periodic payments) over the course of your life (or life expectancy) or the joint lives (or joint life expectancies) of you and your spouse (or whoever is your beneficiary). You are allowed to start this at any age, but you are not allowed to take annuitized distributions from the plan where you currently work. You may only take annuitized payments from a plan at a company where you no longer work.

A Loophole   The drawback to annuitized payments is that they start to deplete your retirement account. Even though payments are calculated according to your life expectancy, however, you may stop taking these withdrawals after five years and reaching age 59 1/2. Then you can stop the distributions and let your money grow again. Obviously, you will not be able to take advantage of this relief if you start annuitized payments long before you are within five years of reaching age 59 1/2.

These periodic payments can be made through a commercial annuity from an insurance company, which would make payments to you and your spouse over your lifetime. Or, you may arrange for annuitized payments according to the schedule called for by the Internal Revenue Service's widely used annuity tables (see Table 5.1).

Also, when you turn 70 1/2 years old, you *must* begin to take payments. Otherwise, you will have to pay a substantial penalty: A 50 percent tax on the minimum amount that should have been distributed.

Triple Threat   If you make an unauthorized early withdrawal from your account, you pay dearly:

- A 20 percent withholding tax. (If you withdraw $10,000, the federal government takes $2,000; you get only $8,000.)

- You pay ordinary income tax on the entire amount. (If you withdraw $10,000, you pay taxes on the whole $10,000 even though you never see $2,000 of it.)

- A 10 percent penalty.

THE PROPER WAY TO TAKE OUT MONEY

There are several ways you can receive your money. Whether you are retiring or leaving your job, you may get it in a lump sum, spread out over time, or transfer it to another tax-deferred account.

There are, however, two important prohibitions:

- Do not take installment payments that add up to more than $150,000 in any single year, even if you've saved enough to be able to do that according to the life expectancy tables. If you do, the IRS will hit the excess amount with a 15 percent penalty in addition to ordinary income taxes.

- Similarly, unless you are transferring your money to another tax-deferred account, do not take a single, lump sum distribution that exceeds $750,000. (Both of these withdrawal limitations are indexed to the cost-of-living, and will rise in the future.)

Here's what you *are* allowed to do if you are leaving your job:

- Ask your current employer if you can leave your account where it is.

- If you can't or don't want to, and if you are taking a new job, see if you can transfer the account to your new workplace. Even if your new workplace offers a 401(k), it may not accept account transfers.

If you do intend to transfer your account, do it directly so money goes from account to account, *not through you*. Otherwise, you may be hit with taxes and penalties on the account. The same warning applies to transferring your money into an IRA if you can't transfer it to a 401(k) at your new workplace (or if you don't like the investment choices in the new plan).

Don't touch the money!   When you move money from one tax-deferred (or "qualified") retirement account into another, don't take personal possession of any of the money. If you do, you'll end up owing taxes on it. Avoid tax liability by 1) Moving the money by making a "transfer," which is when the money is moved directly from one account to another by the custodians; or 2) Establishing a "rollover" Individual Retirement Account (rollover IRA), and moving the money with a check payable to that account—not to you personally. You can either leave it there or move it into another retirement account, perhaps a 401(k) plan at a new job.

If you are retiring:

- You may take a lump sum (but you may want to transfer it into a tax-deferred account like an IRA).

Averaging   If you take a lump sum payment, you may be eligible for a special IRS tax-calculation called "forward averaging" that would let you reduce your overall tax bite. Ask your tax preparer for details.

- You may buy an annuity. (An annuity pays a fixed amount monthly. Whether you buy one yourself or if your employer offers to purchase one for you, shop around. Check for price, payout rates, and the insurer's stability.)

- You may arrange for payments from your account of a set amount of money at intervals, such as once a month, established by your plan. Most companies let you adjust the amount once a year. Some companies even let you treat your account like a savings account, letting you withdraw however much of your balance you want whenever you want.

- You may receive annual distributions from your 401(k) plan. You can do this in either of two ways:

1. **Term certain:** You divide the amount in your nest egg by your life expectancy (alone or as a couple) as predicted by those IRS tables in the year of your retirement (see Table 5.1), and take distributions accordingly. If you retire when both you and your spouse are 65 and both of you are expected to live 25 years, for example, you take 1/25 of your nest egg the first year, 1/24 the second year, 1/23 the third year, and so on.

2. **Recalculation method:** This requires recalculating your life expectancy each year. For example, in your second year of retirement, your life expectancy would be 24.1 years, not 24 as in the "term certain" method. In the third year it would be 23.2 years, not 23. Those small differences would mean you get slightly less in your early years of retirement but the nest egg could last longer—helpful if you happen to live longer!

This chart shows how long the surviving member of a married (or living together) couple is expected to live after his or her spouse dies, at any given age combination. For example, when one spouse is 70 and the other 67, the longer living of the two is expected to survive another 22 years.

Two additional ways of getting your money are through a loan or a "hardship withdrawal." For details on these options, read Lessons 21 and 22.

In this lesson, you learned when you may start to take out your money, and what the penalties are for early withdrawal. In the next lesson, you will learn to understand investment risk.

ACKNOWLEDGMENTS

Input regarding annuitized payments and lump sum distributions: Roy Oliver, National Partner-in-Charge, compensation & benefits, KPMG Peat Marwick.

Input regarding restrictions on the size of distributions: Frank Picarelli, director of The Segal Co.'s defined contributions department.

Input regarding eligibility requirements and annuity rules: David Wray, Profit Sharing/401(k) Council of America.

TABLE 5.1 "LAST SURVIVOR" LIFE-EXPECTANCY CHART

SPOUSE #1

SPOUSE #2

Age	59	60	61	62	63	64	65	66	67	68	69	70	71	72	73	74	75
59	30.6	30.1	29.7	29.3	28.9	28.6	28.2	27.9	27.6	27.4	27.1	26.9	26.7	26.5	26.4	26.2	26.1
60	30.1	29.7	29.2	28.8	28.4	28.0	27.6	27.3	27.0	26.7	26.5	26.2	26.0	25.8	25.6	25.5	25.3
61	29.7	29.2	28.7	28.3	27.8	27.4	27.1	26.7	26.4	26.1	25.8	25.6	25.3	25.1	24.9	24.7	24.6
62	29.3	28.8	28.3	27.8	27.3	26.9	26.5	26.1	25.8	25.5	25.2	24.9	24.7	24.4	24.2	24.0	23.8
63	28.9	28.4	27.8	27.3	26.9	26.4	26.0	25.6	25.2	24.9	24.6	24.3	24.0	23.8	23.5	23.3	23.1
64	28.6	28.0	27.4	26.9	26.4	25.9	25.5	25.1	24.7	24.3	24.0	23.7	23.4	23.1	22.9	22.7	22.4
65	28.2	27.6	27.1	26.5	26.0	25.5	25.0	24.6	24.2	23.8	23.4	23.1	22.8	22.5	22.2	22.0	21.8
66	27.9	27.3	26.7	26.1	25.6	25.1	24.6	24.1	23.7	23.3	22.9	22.5	22.2	21.9	21.6	21.4	21.1
67	27.6	27.0	26.4	25.8	25.2	24.7	24.2	23.7	23.2	22.8	22.4	22.0	21.7	21.3	21.0	20.8	20.5
68	27.4	26.7	26.1	25.5	24.9	24.3	23.8	23.3	22.8	22.3	22.9	21.5	21.2	20.8	20.5	20.2	19.9
69	27.1	26.5	25.8	25.2	24.6	24.0	23.4	22.9	22.4	21.9	21.5	21.1	20.7	20.3	20.0	19.6	19.3
70	26.9	26.2	25.6	24.9	24.3	23.7	23.1	22.5	22.0	21.5	21.1	20.6	20.2	19.8	19.4	19.1	18.8
71	26.7	26.0	25.3	24.7	24.0	23.4	22.8	22.2	21.7	21.2	20.7	20.2	19.8	19.4	19.0	18.6	18.3

continues

TABLE 5.1 CONTINUED

SPOUSE #1

Age	59	60	61	62	63	64	65	66	67	68	69	70	71	72	73	74	75
72	26.5	25.8	25.1	24.4	23.8	23.1	22.5	21.9	21.3	20.8	20.3	19.8	19.4	18.9	18.5	18.2	17.8
73	26.4	25.6	24.9	24.2	23.5	22.9	22.2	21.6	21.0	20.5	20.0	19.4	19.0	18.5	18.1	17.7	17.3
74	26.2	25.5	24.7	24.0	23.3	22.7	22.0	21.4	20.8	20.2	19.6	19.1	18.6	18.2	17.7	17.3	16.9
75	26.1	25.3	24.6	23.8	23.1	22.4	21.8	21.1	20.5	19.9	19.3	18.8	18.3	17.8	17.3	16.9	16.5
76	26.0	25.2	24.4	23.7	23.0	22.3	21.6	20.9	20.3	19.7	19.1	18.5	18.0	17.5	17.0	16.5	16.1
77	25.9	25.1	24.3	23.6	22.8	22.1	21.4	20.7	20.1	19.4	18.8	18.3	17.7	17.2	16.7	16.2	15.8
78	25.8	25.0	24.2	23.4	22.7	21.9	21.2	20.5	19.9	19.2	18.6	18.0	17.5	16.9	16.4	15.9	15.4
79	25.7	24.9	24.1	23.3	22.6	21.8	21.1	20.4	19.7	19.0	18.4	17.8	17.2	16.7	16.1	15.6	15.1
80	26.5	24.8	24.0	23.2	22.4	21.7	21.0	20.2	19.5	18.9	18.2	17.6	17.0	16.4	15.9	15.4	14.9

SPOUSE #2

Source: Internal Revenue Service Publication 939

CALCULATING HOW MUCH TO SAVE

In this lesson, you will learn how to calculate how much money you'll need to save to generate the annual income you want to have after you retire.

How to get what you need depends on what you need. It's one thing to aim for 70, 80, or even 100 percent of your present income (or of the maximum yearly income you expect before retirement). The question is, How large a nest egg will you need to generate that much money every year of your retirement?

In this lesson, you can complete a worksheet that will help you estimate the size nest egg you will need. (In later lessons, you'll learn how to put aside enough money to reach that goal.)

The worksheet leads you step-by-step through a number of calculations involving variables such as your age, pre-retirement salary, number of years to retirement, and level of risk tolerance. For example, the number of years before you retire is important because *time can make money*. It happens mostly in the form of interest, dividends, profits from shares sold and the acquisition of more shares of stock, mutual funds, or whatever units of investment are involved. This growth is measured and described as the rate of return on each of your investments.

> **Rate of Return**   In this book, *rate of return* and *total return* are used interchangeably, unless indicated otherwise, to mean how much an investment has grown. This means a stock, bond, or mutual fund's change in price up or down, plus its interest, dividends, or other income. It is stated as a percentage rate, typically on an annual basis.

The rates of return you may expect in the four categories of investments used for calculations in the worksheet are shown in Table 6.1 below. This table provides conservative estimates for the annual rates of return you may expect for four categories of investments based on their performances over the past 50 years. Use these estimates where indicated in the retirement savings worksheet.

TABLE 6.1   CONSERVATIVE RETURN ESTIMATES

	ANNUAL RETURN ON TAX-DEFERRED INVESTMENTS	RETURN IN 28% BRACKET* FOR NON-DEFERRED INVESTMENTS	RETURN IN 15% BRACKET FOR NON-DEFERRED INVESTMENTS
Small-company stocks	12.0%	8.6%	10.2%
Large-company stocks	10.0%	7.2%	8.5%
Bonds	5.5%	4.0%	4.6%
Cash	3.5%	2.5%	3.0%

* Current top capital-gains tax rate

Source: Maria Crawford Scott, Editor, AAII Journal, *American Ass'n of Individual Investors*

The worksheet makes certain assumptions:

- A four percent rate of inflation

- Your salary will grow at the rate of inflation.

- Your employer's contributions, if any, will also grow at that rate. (The worksheet calculates the total amount or rate at which money must go into your 401(k) account, including any contributions by your employer. If the worksheet indicates you should invest $2,000 a year and your employer contributes $1 for every $1 you contribute, then you personally need to invest only $1,000 of your own money.)

- Your investments are tax-deferred in your 401(k) account. (If you plan to have a lot of additional investments in taxable accounts, do separate calculations for them.)

- Most of your investments are in stocks and low-turnover mutual funds, which will be less affected by capital-gain taxes, than in bonds and Treasury bills.

- You'll be in the same tax bracket after retirement as before.

- You'll use up your savings during retirement.

- Future money is stated in terms of today's dollar value.

- The calculations are conservative, designed so that you will have money left over, rather than underestimating how much you'll need.

Use the worksheet step-by-step, filling in the blanks as needed.

RETIREMENT SAVINGS WORKSHEET

1. YEARLY INCOME IN RETIREMENT:

- How much annual income do you want in retirement? Many financial planners estimate you'll need at least 60% to 80% of current gross salary, so multiply your gross salary by whichever rate makes the most sense to you—perhaps even as high as 100%.

    $_____ Current gross annual income
    ×_____ 60% or more
    = $_____ Desired annual income: **Line 1**

2. OTHER SOURCES OF INCOME:

- How much do you expect to receive annually from other sources like other pension plans or Social Security?

- To obtain an estimate of how much you'll receive from Social Security during retirement, call 1-800-772-1213 and ask for a Request for Earnings and Benefit Estimate Statement. If you expect pension benefits other than your 401(k), ask your benefits or human resources department for an estimate.

- Ask for those estimates to be made in today's dollar values.

    $_____ Annual amount expected from Social Security
    + $_____ Annual amount expected from other sources
    = $_____ Total from other sources: **Line 2**

3. GAP IN DESIRED ANNUAL INCOME:

- Subtract your expected annual benefits in today's dollars from your desired annual income by subtracting Line 2 from Line 1.

- This tells you the amount of annual income you want during retirement that won't be provided by such sources as Social Security.

   $_____ Amount from Line 1
-$_____ Amount from Line 2
= $_____ Result: **Line 3**

4. CLOSING THE GAP—FIRST, DO THIS:

- Find out how big your nest egg will have to be during retirement by multiplying Line 3 by your "annuity factor."

- To find your annuity factor, look at Table 6.2, find the number of years you expect to be in retirement, then go across that row until you find the annual rate of return you expect on your 401(k) savings during retirement. That's based on the annual return column in Table 6.1. Remember, since you'll probably shift to a more cautious and more income-oriented mix of investments after you retire, this will probably be a lower rate of return than during your pre-retirement years.

- For example, if your 401(k) account consists entirely of small-company stocks, you can estimate a 12% annual rate of return. If your account holds only large-company stocks, expect 10%. If your account is split between those two types, figure 11% and so on....

- The number in the column headed by your expected rate of return (in Table 6.2) is your annuity factor.

- The amount on Line 4 of this worksheet tells you how much you'll need to save by retirement to generate the annual income you want, to last the number of years you expect to be in retirement.

$_____ (Line 3)

×_____ Your annuity factor

= $_____ Result: **Line 4**

TABLE 6.2   ANNUITY FACTOR

YEARS RETIRED	EXPECTED ANNUAL RETURN ON SAVINGS				
	4%	6%	8%	10%	12%
20	20.00	16.79	14.31	12.36	10.82
25	25.00	20.08	16.49	13.82	11.80
30	30.00	23.07	18.30	14.93	12.48
35	35.00	25.79	19.79	15.76	12.95
40	40.00	28.26	21.03	16.39	13.28

5. NEXT, TAKE STOCK OF YOUR CURRENT SAVINGS:

- This is how much you have in your 401(k) and any other tax-deferred retirement savings accounts.

$_____ Current Savings: **Line 5**

6. THEN, FIGURE YOUR "SAVINGS GROWTH FACTOR":

- Look at Table 6.3. In the first column, find the number of years until you will retire. Go across that row until you reach the column headed by the annual rate of return you expect on your 401(k) investments before you retire. The number where that row and column intersect is your "Savings Growth Factor."

- Multiply your current savings amount (Line 5) by your Savings Growth Factor.

- The resulting number is how much your savings (without any additions) will grow to by the time you retire if you earn the rate of return you expect to.

- Remember, if you have taxable savings, do these same calculations for them separately below.

$\qquad$ _____ (Line 5)

$\times$_____ Savings Growth Factor

+ \$_____ Result: **Line 6**

TABLE 6.3   SAVINGS GROWTH FACTOR

YEARS TO RETIREMENT	EXPECTED ANNUAL RETURN ON SAVINGS				
	4%	6%	8%	10%	12%
5	1.00	1.10	1.21	1.32	1.45
10	1.00	1.21	1.46	1.75	2.10
15	1.00	1.33	1.76	2.32	3.04
20	1.00	1.46	2.13	3.07	4.40
25	1.00	1.61	2.57	4.06	6.38
30	1.00	1.77	3.10	5.38	9.24
35	1.00	1.95	3.75	7.12	13.38
40	1.00	2.14	4.52	9.43	19.38

7. THE REMAINING SAVINGS SHORTFALL:

* To figure out how much you should save (invest) each year, subtract Line 6 from Line 4.

$\quad$ \$_____ (Line 4)

$\quad$ −\$_____ (Line 6)

$\quad$ = \$_____ Result: **Line 7**

8. ANNUAL SAVINGS:

* Finish the calculation in the step above by finding your "Annual Payment Factor."

* Look at the first column in Table 6.4 to find the number of years until you will retire, and go across that row to the column with your expected rate of return. The corresponding figure is your Annual Payment Factor.

* Multiply Line 7 by your Annual Payment Factor. The result is how much you need to save annually to make up the shortfall in your current savings.

$\quad$ \$_____ (Line 7)

$\quad$ ×_____ Your Annual Payment Factor

$\quad$ = \$_____ Result: **Line 8**

TABLE 6.4 ANNUAL PAYMENT FACTOR

YEARS TO RETIREMENT	EXPECTED ANNUAL RETURN ON SAVINGS				
	4%	6%	8%	10%	12%
5	0.200	0.189	0.178	0.168	0.159
10	0.100	0.090	0.081	0.073	0.065

| YEARS TO | EXPECTED ANNUAL RETURN ON SAVINGS | | | | |
RETIREMENT	4%	6%	8%	10%	12%
15	0.067	0.057	0.049	0.041	0.035
20	0.050	0.041	0.033	0.026	0.021
25	0.040	0.031	0.024	0.018	0.013
30	0.033	0.024	0.018	0.012	0.009
35	0.029	0.020	0.013	0.009	0.006
40	0.025	0.017	0.011	0.006	0.004

9. FINDING YOUR BOTTOM LINE:

- Finally, to convert the annual amount you must invest to make up the shortfall, divide Line 8 by your current salary. (This assumes your salary keeps pace with inflation.) The result is the percentage of your salary you need to save yearly.

  $_____ (Line 8)
  ÷ $_____ Current Salary
  =_____% Result: **Line 9**

10. FIXED DOLLAR AMOUNT TO INVEST:

- Line 9 is a percentage figure that keeps pace with inflation. If, instead, you want to anticipate the cumulative impact of inflation over the course of your working years, you should calculate a fixed dollar amount to contribute annually.

- In Table 6.5, look at the first column, find the number of years until you will retire, and go across that row until the column with the annual rate of return you expect to earn on your 401(k) account before you retire. The corresponding figure is your Fixed Dollar Payment Factor.

• Multiply that figure by your Savings Shortfall (Line 7). The resulting figure is the dollar amount you need to invest each year.

    $_____ (Line 7)
    ×_____ Fixed Dollar Payment Factor
    = $_____ Result: **Dollar Amount to Invest Annually**

Source: Maria Crawford Scott, Editor, AAII Journal, *American Ass'n of Individual Investors*

TABLE 6.5   FIXED DOLLAR ANNUAL PAYMENT FACTOR

YEARS TO RETIREMENT	EXPECTED ANNUAL RETURN ON SAVINGS				
	4%	6%	8%	10%	12%
5	0.225	0.216	0.207	0.199	0.192
10	0.123	0.112	0.102	0.093	0.084
15	0.090	0.077	0.066	0.057	0.048
20	0.074	0.060	0.048	0.038	0.030
25	0.064	0.049	0.036	0.027	0.020
30	0.058	0.041	0.029	0.020	0.013
35	0.054	0.035	0.023	0.015	0.009
40	0.051	0.031	0.019	0.011	0.006

Don't Count Your Chickens   In steps 2 and 3 of the worksheet, when you calculate how much you expect to receive in Social Security, you should not assume that Social Security payments will continue after the year 2013, when the agency forecasts that its spending will exceed its income. Consider making your worksheet calculations twice—once, including possible Social Security benefits, and a second time without including any Social Security benefits.

If the numbers make you flinch, start again, adjusting your assumptions. If you can't afford to invest as much as the worksheet says you'll have to, you have three options:

1. Try to squeeze out a higher rate of return for less money by investing more aggressively.

2. Invest more money for a few years.

3. Think about delaying your retirement.

Whatever you do, start early! Give your money more time to grow.

In this lesson, you learned how to calculate the amount of money you'll need to generate the annual income you want after retirement. In the next lesson, you'll learn how to understand the risks you'll encounter as you accumulate your nest egg.

ACKNOWLEDGMENTS

The worksheet with tables in this lesson is adapted with permission from one created by Maria Crawford Scott, editor of the *AAII Journal*, published by the American Association of Individual Investors.

UNDERSTANDING RISK

In this lesson, you will learn what types of risks your investments face.

Now that you know how to calculate how much money you'll need for retirement, you need to understand the risks you'll encounter accumulating this nest egg. Then, you can learn how to cope with those risks so you can reach your retirement goal.

Generally, as an investor you must beware of four kinds of risk:

- **Business risk**
- **Interest risk**
- **Market risk**
- **Inflation risk**

WHAT DO THEY MEAN, ANYWAY?

If you can predict the four kinds of risk reliably, you end up with far more money than you'll ever need. If you're like most people, though, you're lucky if you can predict them even a small fraction of the time.

Business risk   This is the risk that's probably easiest to understand. If a company is in danger of going out of business or operating less profitably, it's a bad risk.

Interest risk   Interest is the price of money, and like anything else it's a price that rises and falls. Banks, for example, charge people interest for loans. Interest rates change all the time, and as they go up or down they drag the value of certain investments up or down with them. After all, who wants a CD that pays 5 percent when you can get one for 7 percent?

Market risk   Even if a company is run by geniuses whose talent is exceeded only by that of their dedicated work force, the larger economy can intervene by taking a dive. After all, did *you* foresee the stock market crash of 1987? Overnight, markets disappear, money for loans evaporates, supplies get cut off. Profits plunge. A year or two passes before new customers are found. Meanwhile, a company's stock goes into the hopper. Can you weather it?

Inflation risk   Inflation corrodes the value of money you earn and save. The dollar that buys you a can of soup now bought five or six cans when Eisenhower was President. It will buy even less by the time you retire. You must measure the value of your investments by their return adjusted for the rate of inflation.

APPLYING THIS TO YOUR 401(K) PLAN

The trouble with risk is that it does not affect all investments in the same way. Nor does it affect all investors the same way.

Businesses are vulnerable to different risks and they are vulnerable to risks in varying degrees. Likewise, some investors are better positioned to handle certain kinds of risks than others, and something that threatens one investor may not faze another investor as much.

Often, risk boils down to a matter of time. If you have 10 or 20 years to go until retirement, you have a lot more time to bounce back from an investment setback than someone who will retire in one year.

You have to know which investments are riskier than others—especially to you, in the time you have before retirement.

In general, over the course of decades, small-company stocks have shown the most risk. It's not that they lose the most money—in fact, just the opposite. A dollar invested in small-company stocks at the end of 1925 would have grown to $2,842.77 by the end of 1994.* That's more than the $800.08 it would have grown to in large-company stocks or any of several other categories of investments.*

The trouble with small-company stocks is their wide swings. Those small-company stocks rewarded their investors with a total annual return of almost 143 percent in 1933.* But they also plummeted 58 percent in 1937.*

Their unpredictability, as measured by those one-year swings, gives investors a wilder ride with greater ups and downs than other categories of Wall Street investments.

That's their risk.

Another way time may pose a risk to your investments is through inflation. The power of inflation to erode your savings and investments is often overlooked, so let's take a closer look at it.

Let's say you're 35 years old and you're willing to invest $3,500 a year towards retirement. You put your money into several stock-based mutual funds and, using a common yardstick, you expect to earn 10 percent a year on your investments.

By retirement-age 65 your investments will swell to more than $575,000. Better yet, going by IRS life-expectancy tables that say you'll probably live another 20 years after reaching 65, that nest egg will hatch more than $55,000 a year for you to live on. That assumes you're in the 28 percent tax bracket during retirement and, quite naturally, that the money stays invested and continues to grow.

But the Real World Treats You Differently

In the real world, your $575,000 nest egg is worth only $177,508 in today's dollars after inflation eats away at it. That provides you with only $12,500 a year after retirement.

On the other hand, inflation may help you at the same time it erodes your earnings. Let's say your pay rises at the same 4 percent rate as inflation. Now your nest egg is worth almost $829,000 at retirement. Inflation whittles that down to a little more than $255,000 in today's buying power. That will produce slightly less than $18,000 a year from age 65 to 85, after taxes.

However, what happens if inflation stays at 3.5 percent rather than a full 4 percent? The same $3,500 annual investment grows into more than $788,000—less than before—but it's worth more! Inflation erodes it only to about $281,000. That will generate better than $20,500 after retirement.

THE NUMBERS GAME

You can see now that different risks carry different penalties. But they can be sized up. Then, once you know what you're up against, you can form your strategy.

In this lesson, you learned how to understand risk. In the next lesson, you will begin to learn how to cope with various risks.

ACKNOWLEDGMENTS

Calculations involving compound growth of investments and effects of inflation on retirement finances done with Managing Your Money, a personal-finance program from MECA Software, in Fairfield, Conn.

*Source: ©*Stocks, Bonds, Bills, and Inflation 1995 Yearbook*™, Ibbotson Associates, Chicago (annually updates work by Roger G. Ibbotson and Rex A. Sinquefield). Used by permission. All rights reserved.

COPING WITH RISK: FIRST TACTIC

In this lesson, you will learn that the first defense against investment risk is to minimize it through diversification.

In Lesson 7, you learned how different risks threaten your investments. In this lesson you will learn the first of several ways to cope with those risks.

Your most basic defense against investment risk is to minimize it. You should follow the old adage, "Don't put all your eggs in one basket."

When it comes to investment, staying away from trouble is a matter of applying a technique called *diversification*: don't expose all of your money to a single risk. As a defense against risk, this is the most important precaution you can take. By diversifying, you spread your risk. By spreading your investments, you reduce the chances that all your investments will go down at the same time.

Basically, there are two ways you should diversify:

- **Put your money into different types of assets.**
  Instead of investing only in stocks or stock-based
  mutual funds, invest in bond or bond funds as well.

  Most 401(k) plans make this easy to do by offering
  you at least three investment options. To comply
  with federal 401(k) plan rules, those options are supposed to represent different levels of risk, so they will
  be different types and styles of investment assets.

- **Spread your money within an asset category.**
  Don't buy the stock of only one company or industry.
  Don't even buy only Blue Chip stocks or stock funds.
  Buy small-company stocks or stock funds to balance
  those large-company investments. If you buy a mutual fund whose focus is a particular industry, balance
  it by buying a fund whose stocks will not be affected
  by the same risks.

For example, the value of a mutual fund that holds stock in
real estate investments may decline when interest rates go up
because fewer people can afford to buy homes. If you own a
mutual fund that specializes in real estate, balance it with a
fund that's less sensitive to interest rate fluctuations, like one
specializing in food-processing companies—people eat even
when interest rates rise!

Advocates of aggressive investment strategies would advise you
to interpret these rules liberally, especially if you're young and
have lots of time to nurture your investments. In other words,
don't put a lot of money into bonds or bond funds if you're
young. Time should enable you to weather any short-term
fluctuations in the stock market as well as diversifying into
bonds would.

If you're older—especially if you are approaching or in retirement—and need steady income from stable principal, then the rule about diversifying between bonds and stocks is more important. Diversifying within asset categories, however, is sound advice no matter what age you are.

One tactic you should avoid at any age is market-timing.

Forget Market-Timing   *Market-timing* is a strategy that means the same thing as buying low, selling high. The trouble is, it's difficult even for Wall Street professionals to get it right. The markets move too fast and too often, for you to be able to buy at the lowest price and sell at the highest price. If you try, you'll end up missing your targets and wasting your money on transaction fees.

Market-timing is, in many ways, the opposite of diversification. Rather than spreading your risk, market-timing requires you to focus your risk by betting heavily on one or more investments.

Successful investing takes time and patience. Market-timing pretends that investing is easy and can bring success overnight. Beware: Market-timing is the Wall Street version of fool's gold.

In this lesson, you learned that the first defense against investment risk is to minimize it through diversification. In the next lesson, you will learn how to use time as another defense against risk.

COPING WITH RISK: SECOND TACTIC

In this lesson, you will learn another valuable defense against investment risk: time.

The simplest defense is to start investing early. Just as time can work against you—in the form of inflation—time can work in your favor, too. By starting early, you give your money a chance to grow.

One way it does that is through a process called *compounding*. Compounding may happen at intervals such as quarterly, monthly, weekly, even daily. Whatever the interval, the longer you keep your money invested, the more it earns.

 Compounding Compounding happens when you earn interest on your original investment as well as on the interest itself. For example, if you deposit $1,000 in a bank account that earns 10 percent interest, you will have $1,100 at the end of the first year. Both your original $1,000 and the extra $100 earn 10 percent interest—another $10—during the next year, so by the end of the second year you have $1,210.

The same process can work on stocks, bonds, and mutual funds. The compounding may take the form of money, dividends, or new shares of stock or a mutual fund that you plow back into your account.

Another way to look at it is that the earlier you start, the less money you'll need to take out of each of your paychecks to build whatever size retirement nest egg you're aiming for.

Table 9.1 shows what happens to three people with different investment strategies, each earning the same hypothetical 10 percent annual rate of return.

Each person invests $2,000 a year. Employee #1 starts at age 25 and invests $2,000 only for the first 10 years, making no additional investments for the next 30 years, but leaving the existing account in place, earning 10 percent each of the next 30 years. By the time Employee #1 retires at 65, he or she has invested only $20,000, but this sum has ballooned to $672,998 over the 30 years.

Employee #3 does not start investing until age 35, but then diligently continues for the next 30 years. Incredibly, even though this person invests three times more money— $60,000—and does it for triple the amount of time as Employee #1, he or she ends up with less money: only $400,276!

Employee #1's 10-year head start makes all the difference because the money is compounding and building on itself for more time.

Of course, Employee #2 enjoys the best of all worlds at retirement age by starting at age 25 and continuing for the full 40 years. His nest egg mushrooms into more than $1 million.

Table 9.1 also shows how much extra money each gets by working an additional two years. (Early next century, the eligibility age for Social Security is scheduled to rise to 67 from 65.)

TABLE 9.1   THE POWER OF COMPOUNDING

AGE	EMPLOYEE #1's ANNUAL CONTRIBUTION	INVESTMENTS' CUMULATIVE VALUE AT YEAR'S END	EMPLOYEE #2's ANNUAL CONTRIBUTION	INVESTMENTS' CUMULATIVE VALUE AT YEAR'S END	EMPLOYEE #3's ANNUAL CONTRIBUTION	INVESTMENTS' CUMULATIVE VALUE AT YEAR'S END
25	$2,000	$2,200	$2,000	$2,200		
26	2,000	4,620	2,000	4,620		
27	2,000	7,282	2,000	7,282		
28	2,000	10,210	2,000	10,210		
29	2,000	13,431	2,000	13,431		
30	2,000	16,974	2,000	16,974		
31	2,000	20,872	2,000	20,872		
32	2,000	25,159	2,000	25,159		
33	2,000	29,875	2,000	29,875		
34	2,000	35,062	2,000	35,062		
35		38,569	2,000	40,769	$2,000	$2,200
36		42,425	2,000	47,045	2,000	4,620
37		46,668	2,000	53,950	2,000	7,282
38		51,335	2,000	61,545	2,000	10,210
39		56,468	2,000	69,899	2,000	13,431
40		62,115	2,000	79,089	2,000	16,974
41		68,327	2,000	89,198	2,000	20,872

42	75,159	2,000	100,318	2,000	25,159
43	82,675	2,000	112,550	2,000	29,875
44	90,943	2,000	126,005	2,000	35,062
45	100,037	2,000	140,805	2,000	40,769
46	110,041	2,000	157,086	2,000	47,045
47	121,045	2,000	174,995	2,000	53,950
48	133,149	2,000	194,694	2,000	61,545
49	146,464	2,000	216,364	2,000	69,899
50	161,110	2,000	240,200	2,000	79,089
51	177,222	2,000	266,420	2,000	89,198
52	194,944	2,000	295,262	2,000	100,318
53	214,438	2,000	326,988	2,000	112,550
54	235,882	2,000	361,887	2,000	126,005
55	259,470	2,000	400,276	2,000	140,805
56	285,417	2,000	442,503	2,000	157,086
57	313,959	2,000	488,953	2,000	174,995
58	345,355	2,000	540,049	2,000	194,694
59	379,890	2,000	596,254	2,000	216,364

continues

TABLE 9.1 CONTINUED

AGE	EMPLOYEE #1's ANNUAL CONTRIBUTION	INVESTMENTS' CUMULATIVE VALUE AT YEAR'S END	EMPLOYEE #2's ANNUAL CONTRIBUTION	INVESTMENTS' CUMULATIVE VALUE AT YEAR'S END	EMPLOYEE #3's ANNUAL CONTRIBUTION	INVESTMENTS' CUMULATIVE VALUE AT YEAR'S END
60		417,879	2,000	658,079	2,000	240,200
61		459,667	2,000	726,087	2,000	266,420
62		505,634	2,000	800,896	2,000	295,262
63		556,197	2,000	883,185	2,000	326,988
64		611,817	2,000	973,704	2,000	361,887
65		672,998	2,000	1,073,274	2,000	400,276
66		740,298	2,000	1,182,801	2,000	442,503
67		$814,328	2,000	$1,303,282	2,000	$488,953

TOTAL INVESTMENT:

EMPLOYEE #1	EMPLOYEE #2	EMPLOYEE #3
$20,000	$86,000	$66,000

Source: Dee Lee, Harvard Financial Educators

Here's another way to look at how much of an advantage Employee #1 has by starting early. If Employee #3 wants to catch up, he or she must contribute $3,331 a year—more than half-again as much as Employee #1's $2,000 annual investment—to end up with the same $814,328 at age 67. And Employee #3 must do that for a full 32 years, in comparison to Employee #1, who contributed for only 10 years.

That's the tremendous advantage that time provides. It lets your nest egg grow bigger.

In this lesson, you learned that the second defense against investment risk is to give time a chance to make your money grow. In the next lesson, you will learn the third defense against risk.

ACKNOWLEDGMENTS

Compounding calculations: Dee Lee, Harvard Financial Educators.

10

COPING WITH RISK: THIRD TACTIC

In this lesson, you will learn another way to put time to work for you as a defense against investment risk.

One other way you can use time to your advantage is by putting the long-term trend of businesses to grow and generate profits to work for you. The longer you invest for, the better you'll do.

Investing over a long time period helps you overcome the risks you learned about in Lesson 7, including the two most dramatic: business risk and market risk. Businesses do not succeed all the time, of course. The fortunes of individual businesses, and of the stock market overall, go up and down, sometimes spectacularly. Moreover, some categories of businesses suffer wilder, more unpredictable fluctuations than others.

Categories of business that provide the best total return over time are also the riskiest in the short-run. That means they may produce the best total return over the course of many years, but in brief spans of time their performance fluctuates wildly up and down.

FOCUSING IN

Here's a more detailed look at the levels of risk of different business categories.

Small American businesses have been the most risky category of investment in this country. Next have been foreign companies, followed by large American companies, which in turn are riskier than intermediate-term government bonds (bonds that reach *maturity*, or payoff, in five years) and riskier still than Treasury bills.*

This risk is measured in terms of *volatility*—the wildness of the fluctuations up and down in what an investor gets out of a stock or bond (its *return*: its price change plus dividends or interest). These fluctuations can be measured for any period of time, such as a single year.

Small-company stocks, for example, rewarded their investors with a total return of almost 143 percent in 1933. But they also plummeted 58 percent in 1937.*

The best single year for large-company stocks was their 54 percent total return in 1933, in comparison to their worst year, which was 1931, when their total return plunged 43.3 percent.*

But that volatility diminishes dramatically as you measure the average annual peaks and valleys over time periods longer than one year.

If you look at any 10-year period, for instance, the best annual performance for small companies averages 30.38 percent, while the worst annual average is -5.7 percent.* That's a much less wild swing from best to worst than for the single-year performances.

The fluctuation from best to worst is smoother still when you look at 20-year periods. Then, the best annual performance averages out to 21.13 percent, while the average worst yearly performance (technically, the worst "compound average annual total return") is 5.74 percent, no longer even in negative numbers.*

The longer the period of time over which the average is measured, the milder the roller-coaster ride becomes for an investor. The peaks get shorter, while the valleys no longer are so deep. The same holds true for any business category.

That's the advantage of putting time to work for you.

RECOVERY MAY BE SWIFT

Often, time heals quickly. After the October 1987 stock market crash, when the Dow Jones Industrial Average, a popular measurement of stock market performance, plunged more than 500 points in a single session, it took the market only 15 months to recover. It took merely one more month for the market to advance 5 percent beyond where it had been before the Crash. In other words, an investor who waited a mere 16 months after the Crash of '87 not only weathered the storm but enjoyed a 5 percent gain.

Over longer periods of time, returns on investments are even greater.

If you are a baby boomer who finished high school, college, or graduate school in the late 1960s or early '70s, got a job, and saved enough to invest $10,000 by 1975, here's how you would have done by holding onto that investment for 20 years:

- If you had invested in a typical small-company mutual fund, your $10,000 would have grown into $220,663 by 1995. If you had invested in the Achievement fund group's Acorn Fund, which was the most successful small-company fund during that period, your $10,000 would have ballooned into $363,530.

- Similarly, if you had invested in a typical mutual fund investing in medium-size companies, your $10,000 would have grown into $231,484.

- Or, if you had invested in a typical so-called growth category mutual fund, which is the type that invests largely in the stocks of Blue Chip companies—large American corporations—your $10,000 would have grown into $191,977.

- However, funds in the growth category had a very wide range of performances from best to worst. The average annual rate of return for the *category* was just short of 15 percent, producing that $191,977 lump sum. But if you had put your money into any of the five best *individual* funds in this group, it would have grown into as much as $978,986 (in comparison to Acorn's $363,530).

To put those performances into perspective, compare them to the following:

- The Consumer Price Index, which the federal government uses to measure changes in the cost-of-living, almost tripled during that two-decade period. If you had spent $10,000 on the living costs measured by the CPI in 1975, those same living costs would have cost $28,135 in 1995.

- Or, if you had invested $10,000 in a mutual fund imitating the performance of the Standard & Poor's 500-stock index (which is a group of stocks commonly used to measure the stock market's overall performance), that investment would have grown into $145,438 by 1995.

You could also interpret those performances by noting that while the Acorn Fund grew more than 35-fold in those 20 years, the CPI grew about 1.8 times and the S&P 500's total return grew more than 13-fold. An investment in the Acorn Fund would have kept you well ahead of the ever-increasing pace of the cost-of-living.

Taken together, these comparisons teach you three important rules:

- Investing long-term, the gains of even the riskiest categories of stocks and mutual funds outweigh the losses, dramatically increasing your potential to earn money.

- The riskiest categories of stocks and mutual funds produce gains that far outstrip the steep pace of inflation, reflected in the upward creep of the cost of living.

- The longer your investment time period, the safer you are and the better you stand to do!

In this lesson, you learned a second way of putting time to work for yourself as a defense against investment risk. In the next lesson, you will learn the first step in selecting investments that best suit your needs.

ACKNOWLEDGMENTS

Mutual-fund, Consumer Price Index, and S&P 500 data: Lipper Analytical Services.

*Source: ©*Stocks, Bonds, Bills, and Inflation 1995 Yearbook*™, Ibbotson Associates, Chicago (annually updates work by Roger G. Ibbotson and Rex A. Sinquefield). Used by permission. All rights reserved.

11

FIND OUT YOUR RISK TOLERANCE

In this lesson, you will learn how much risk you can tolerate in your investments.

SEEK THE CORRECT BALANCE

If a long investment period—your "time horizon"—can produce the sizzling results discussed in Lessons 9 and 10, you may be wondering if you should simply invest in the riskiest categories, sit back, and wait.

The answer is no. Not automatically, anyway. One reason is that you may not have a long period of time before you need your money back. You may be only a few years away from retirement, for example. Another reason is that not every company, stock, bond, or mutual fund will do well over time. The odds may favor certain *categories* of investments over others, but any *individual* investment is still subject to setbacks, even outright collapse.

All investments are subject to risk. Even if you select an investment for the long term, you could lose your money if the investment declines substantially even for a relatively short period.

Therefore, what you select as your investment depends not only on your time horizon but also on how much risk you can handle before you start to lose sleep at night.

Risk Tolerance   The amount of danger or volatility you can tolerate in your investments. It will vary according to such variables as your circumstances, age, income, financial resources, and amount of time before you need to use your money.

Although you may think the solution is simply to select the most risk-free investment strategy available, this means you'll lose out on potential rewards. The more risk you take, the higher your potential rewards. The safer you play it, the lower your investment return is likely to be.

Instead, you should aim for the best total return from your investments by figuring out the highest level of risk you can tolerate. Once you determine your risk-tolerance, you'll know better whether to pursue a cautious, moderate, or aggressive investment strategy. Within any of those strategies, you can custom-tailor investments as much as possible to suit your individual needs.

YOUR RISK TOLERANCE WILL CHANGE

Your risk tolerance will probably change as you get older. When you're younger, you have more years to recover from a dip in the value of your investments. When you retire, you need to count on a certain annual income from your nest egg to pay your bills—no matter what. As you approach retirement age, you'll probably want to shift from an aggressive strategy to an increasingly cautious one.

In addition to your age, your risk tolerance is determined by your income, job security, prospects for career advancement, marital status, number of children, and non-retirement goals such as whether you want to buy a boat or a second home.

To help you pinpoint your present risk tolerance, take the quiz in Table 11.1. At the end, add up the points for each answer and see which investment style your score corresponds to. This multiple-choice quiz will help you figure out how much risk you are willing to take with your investment money. Not all of the questions are about 401(k) plan investments, but they are all geared to casting light on your attitude toward taking financial risks. Add up the points for each answer to find your score—and your risk-tolerance profile.

TABLE 11.1   RISK TOLERANCE

1. How many years before you retire?

   (1 point) Less than five

   (2 points) Five to 10

   (3 points) 10 to 20

   (4 points) More than 20

   Your answer:

2. How many adults in your household earn an income?

   (1) One

   (2) Two

   Your answer:

3. If you inherited $30,000, how would you invest it?

   (1) Treasury bills

   (2) Certificates of deposit

   (3) A mutual fund that holds bonds

   (4) A mutual fund that holds stock in Blue Chip and other large businesses

   (5) A mutual fund that invests in only one industry

   Your answer:

4. You have financial assets like a non-401(k) pension plan or personal savings (but excluding your home and Social Security) that will contribute how much to your income during retirement?

   (1) Probably not much.

   (2) One-third of the income you'll need.

   (3) More than half of what you'll need.

   Your answer:

5. Which statement best describes the savings you have outside your 401(k) plan?

   (1) "What savings?"

   (2) "It pays for monthly bills."

   (3) "It not only pays for monthly bills but also for vacations and emergencies."

   (4) "I have several accounts, some for monthly bills, some for expenses like my kids' college educations."

   Your answer:

6. Your rich uncle, who is as honest as a saint, offers you several investment deals. Which do you do?

   (1) Invest $1,000 so you can get back $1,100 at the end of a year?

(2) Invest $1,000 with a 50-50 chance you'll lose it all or get $1,750 at the end of a year?

(3) Invest $2,000 with a 50-50 chance you'll lose it all or get back $4,000 at the end of a year?

Your answer:

7. Which is closest to the biggest chance you ever took?

    (1) Playing the state lottery.

    (2) Gambling in a casino.

    (3) Quitting your job to start your own business.

    Your answer:

8. Two-thirds of your 401(k) money is in stock mutual funds, the rest is in bond mutual funds. This week the stock market went into a tailspin and your stock funds lost 15 percent of their value. What do you do next?

    (1) Cut your losses by transferring your money into the bond funds.

    (2) Keep your money where it is and wait for the market to turn around.

    (3) Invest more money in the stock funds, because their prices are such a good deal now.

    Your answer:

9. Two-thirds of your 401(k) money is in stock mutual funds, the rest is in bond mutual funds. Yesterday the stock market went into a tailspin and your stock funds lost 15 percent of their value. What did you do last night?

    (1) You did not sleep well.

    (2) Thought about the last time the market crashed and tried to remember how long it took your investments to recover.

(3) Made a mental note to look for bargain investments in the business pages of this morning's newspaper.

Your answer:

10. If you get laid off, you have enough savings outside your 401(k) plan to cover living expenses for how long?

    (1) Up to three months

    (2) Up to six months

    (3) Up to nine months

    (4) More than nine months

    Your answer:

11. Your hometown football team is undefeated going into their next-to-last game of the season. They are about to play a team that has not won a game all season. You have a chance to bet $200 on your home team, with a chance to win $400.

    (1) Who cares. You don't gamble.

    (2) You split the cost of the bet with one of your friends.

    (3) You make the bet with your own money.

    (4) You borrow the $200 from that rich uncle, but win or lose you've got to repay him $220 in one week.

    Your answer:

12. You are 35 years old and have just inherited $1 million. You decide to:

    (1) Buy a new home.

    (2) Quit your job and go back to school.

    (3) Keep your job and go back to school.

    Your answer:

Total points:

Now, to determine your level of risk-tolerance, add up your points.

- **If you scored 12 to 20 points:**

  You are probably a conservative investor. You cannot tolerate risk well and should pursue a strategy that avoids risk by putting your money into investments that sacrifice higher potential return for the sake of predictability and safety.

  Your investment motto: **Better safe than sorry.**

- **If you scored 21 to 36 points:**

  You seem to be a moderate-risk investor. Your answers indicate you prefer limited risk that will not expose your investments to unknown hazards. You are probably the sort of investor who is willing to seek higher investment returns by taking chances, but only highly calculated ones.

  Your investment motto: **One step at a time.**

- **If you scored 37 to 41 points:**

  You come across as an aggressive investor. You seem comfortable taking risks to seek higher returns. You've indicated sufficient concern for your financial future to engage in some investment planning. Where some investors see danger, you see investment bargains.

  Your investment motto: **No pain, no gain.**

Now that you know what sort of investor you are, the next step is to shape an investment strategy that suits you.

In this lesson, you learned how much risk you can tolerate in your investments. In the next lesson, you will learn how to use your risk tolerance to choose your investments.

12

ASSET ALLOCATION

In this lesson, you will learn how to translate your level of risk tolerance into a practical investment strategy.

Now that you know what your risk-tolerance level is, you can select appropriate investment options. The more aggressive you are as an investor, the more risk you'll accept in your investments.

Investments cover a risk spectrum. Generally, the safest provide the lowest rates of return. The least-risky investments are called *cash equivalents*, like money market funds and Treasury bills (which are *debt obligations*, or IOUs, from the federal govern-ment).* Next in line are some *fixed-income investments*, such as government bonds and corporate bonds, which are longer-term debt obligations.* Farther out on the branch of safety are *large-company stocks* (and mutual funds based on that stock), followed by *international companies* and, finally, *small companies*.*

Safety Here, safety is defined in terms of your *principal* or initial cash investment being unlikely to lose short-term value. A different way of defining safety is in terms of your investment's ability to stay ahead of inflation, maintaining its long-term value. (See Lesson 13.)

Here is how to select the right combination of investments for you. Your choices are likely to consist of so-called cash equivalents, mutual funds, and stock in your own company.

- **Stock**   Shares of stock represent ownership of a corporation. Generally, the portion you own is relative to a company's total amount of stock. For example, if you own 1,000 shares of a company that has issued 1 million shares, you own one-tenth of one percent. The price of shares may rise or fall. Also, the company may distribute all or part of its profits to shareholders for each share they own. Those payments are called *dividends*.

- **Mutual fund**   A fund managed by investment professionals who pool peoples' money and invest it in stocks, bonds, and other securities. Like an individual company's stock, the price of mutual fund shares is determined by dividing the number of shares into the market value of everything in which the fund has invested. All the securities owned by the fund are called its *portfolio*.

- **Cash equivalent**   A loan to some borrower that is extremely likely to repay the debt within the agreed-upon short time period. Thus, the loan agreement is as good as having cash. Cash equivalents include money market funds, bank certificates of deposit, Treasury bills, and GICs (or Guaranteed Investment Contracts). The terms *GIC fund* and *stable value fund* are sometimes used interchangeably.

- **Bond**   Similar to a cash equivalent, a bond is also a loan to a borrower that promises to pay back the loan itself (the *principal*) plus interest. Unlike stock, it does not represent ownership of the company. One difference between a bond and a cash equivalent is that a bond is much more complex and its principal may grow or shrink.

Next, bear in mind that choices will be limited. Your plan will probably offer you at least three choices, each representing a different balance between risk and reward, to comply with certain federal pension laws. Three to six or more choices is a common range.

Here is what each type does, its pros and cons:

TYPES OF LOANS

- **Cash equivalent**   A short-term loan to a borrower.

   Pros: Generally the lowest risk investment in the short term. Usually easy to convert to cash (known as *liquidity*). Easy-to-understand interest rate or rate of return. Good place to put money you might need to get your hands on quickly.

   Cons: Your principal does not grow, and their interest rates barely keep pace with inflation. Inflation sometimes exceeds their interest rate so they're not good for long-term investments. Inside your 401(k) plan, their liquidity is reduced. In GICs, the word "Guaranteed" should not be misunderstood: it is merely a promise from an insurance company, not the federal government, and on rare occasions such insurers have actually failed to repay the principal or pay the promised interest rate.

- **"Fixed-income" investment**   Tells you what interest rate or "yield" it intends to pay. This category consists of a wide range of government and private-business bonds and bond mutual funds (as well as certain stocks that pay a set dividend). They are like IOUs for a specified period of time (known as the *term*).

Risk varies according to the underlying borrower's ability to repay your loan. Government bonds are usually safer than corporate bonds. Bonds described as *investment grade* are safer than others. Several rating services grade bonds according to the borrower's ability to repay. Usually, borrowers with lower credit ratings pay higher interest rates. Also, the longer the bond's term, the more interest a borrower usually must pay.

A key difference between a bond and a bond fund is this: A bond pays a fixed yield until its date of maturity, but a bond fund's interest may vary because the fund is constantly buying and selling bonds whose yields may differ. So, don't count on a bond fund always paying what it does initially.

Pros: Rate of return usually higher than on cash equivalents. Steady income with relative safety for principal.

Cons: Rate of return usually lower than on stocks and stock funds. These are more complex investments than cash equivalents. For one thing, the principal itself may grow or shrink as interest rates fall or climb. Thus, you have to judge a bond or bond fund by its *total return*—its interest rate plus the bond or fund's price. The longer its term, the more volatile the bond or fund; long-term bonds or funds may suffer dramatic losses in principal value, even if they are government bonds offering a high yield.

SOME TYPES OF STOCKS AND STOCK FUNDS

- **Growth**   Invests in companies whose earnings are expected to grow faster than average. Rising or falling earnings drive the value of stock held by the fund and the fund's own price per share up or down.

  Growth funds (and Growth & Income funds) are the closest thing to a category of mutual funds that invests in large corporations, although they are not restricted to large-company investments.

  Pros & cons: Over long periods of time, successful growth funds generally far exceed the rate of inflation. You pay for that high rate of return, however, with a lot of short-term volatility that makes these funds risky. During any short period, the value of your principal could decline.

- **Growth & Income**   This is a fund that invests mostly in large corporations with steady earnings and dividends, seeking growth from rising share price (from the earnings) and income (from the dividends).

  This category may include *index* funds that invest in the companies that make up the Dow Jones Industrial Average or the Standard & Poor's 500-stock index. Those are baskets (or *portfolios*) of Blue Chip stocks, used to calculate the stock market's performance. The manager of an index fund simply imitates the stock holdings of a certain index rather than creating an independent investment strategy. Not all G&I funds are index funds.

Pros & cons: An investment that provides income usually does so at the expense of growth of principal over time. Over the long term, this category has slightly less total return than the growth category.

- **Balanced**   These funds invest in both stocks and bonds.

Pros & cons: Investing in both stocks and bonds provides safety and stability. Bond prices are more sensitive to the borrowing-price of money than to many other general stock market conditions and don't rise as fast as stock prices in a rising stock market. Therefore, a balanced fund's total return won't rise as much as a stock fund's during a rising market. On the other hand, income from interest and dividends from its bonds will help a balanced fund do better than an all-stock fund during a falling stock market.

- **Sector**   A fund that specializes in one or more related industries such as real estate, financial services, or biotechnology.

Pros & cons: Like any less-diversified investment, sector funds are subject to sharp fluctuations in total return. They are a risky short-term investment.

- **Small-company**   Also known as small capitalization (*small cap*) or small-company growth funds, these funds invest in the stock of small companies.

Pros & cons: These funds are risky because of short-term volatility but they offer the best long-term return of any fund category.

- **International fund**   Invests in stocks of companies outside the U.S.

  Pro: Foreign stock markets may not rise and fall in lock-step with the American stock market, so a stable international fund can cushion your 401(k) account during a falling domestic market.

  Con: One danger to international funds is currency-exchange risk. If the foreign currency rises in value, your fund's shares are worth more. But if the currency falls in comparison to dollars, your investment is worth less.

  International funds should not be confused with "global funds," which may invest in businesses anywhere on the globe, including the U.S.

- **Lifestyle**   A lifestyle fund invests in a mix of investments that otherwise would not be in a fund together.

  Pro: Rather than making you select different funds to find the balance of risk and return that you're comfortable with, a lifestyle or "asset-allocation" fund does it for you.

  Con: Like any fund with built-in cushions against stock market setbacks, lifestyle funds sacrifice potential gain for safety. Also, the fund's prefabricated mix of investments may not suit your needs exactly.

- **Company stock**   Company stock is the second most popular option (after fixed-income investments like bond funds and GICs) in 401(k) plans. Some companies make their matching contribution as company stock instead of cash.

Pros & cons: The benefit of investing in company stock is that it's a business you're familiar with. It's also risky, however, because both your current income and your retirement nest egg are then vulnerable to the ups and downs of one company. If you have other options, it's worth considering them to spread your risk.

FINDING THE RIGHT FIT

Now that you know about the differences among various types of investments, it's time to learn about mixing and matching different types of investments to suit your preferences.

You took the first step towards that in Lesson 11, where you learned what your risk-tolerance level or profile is (conservative/low risk; moderate/medium risk; aggressive/high risk). Now, find your age group and risk-tolerance level in Table 12.1, then see what mix of investments is appropriate for you. The chart indicates how you may divide your 401(k) plan investment money.

Most of your 401(k) plan investment choices will be mutual funds, so find the *asset allocation*—or mix of mutual fund categories—that suits your age and level of risk-tolerance.

If, for example, you're a twentysomething who recognizes that you have little to lose and lots of time to recover from setbacks, you may be comfortable loading up on mutual funds that invest in small domestic businesses and foreign businesses, both volatile categories with high potential rewards. The 20 percent of your money that you put into mutual funds investing in large American corporations would be the conservative portion of your 401(k) account.

TABLE 12.1   ASSET ALLOCATION

AGE AND RISK-TOLERANCE	SMALL COMPANIES	INTERNATIONAL BUSINESSES	LARGE COMPANIES	BALANCED	BONDS/ GICs	MONEY-MARKET FUND(s)
In Your 20s						
Low	20%	25%	55%			
Moderate	30%	10%	40%	20%		
High	50%	30%	20%			
In Your 30s						
Low	10%	15%	5%	35%	30%	5%
Moderate	25%	20%	55%			
High	50%	30%	20%			
In Your 40s						
Low	5%	5%	5%	35%	35%	15%
Moderate	5%	10%	20%	55%	10%	
High	40%	30%	20%	10%		
In Your 50s						
Low	5%	5%	5%	15%	35%	35%
Moderate	20%	25%	55%			
High	20%	20%	40%	10%	10%	

At the other end of the spectrum, people in their 50s, approaching retirement, would probably be most at ease with an asset allocation that puts most of their money into mutual funds that expose the principal—the nest egg—to the least short-term danger, even if that strategy requires sacrificing some potential total return on the investment dollar.

Look at the first row of that age group: Truly conservative investors—let's say in their late 50s, on the threshold of retirement, with low risk-tolerance—might well put 70 percent of their money into categories filled with bonds and cash-equivalent investments. The balanced mutual funds, where these investors put 15 percent of their money, also hold bonds.

Thanks to a combination of investment selection and compounding, over time these asset allocations produce very different results.

The twentysomething investor makes out best, even if he or she chooses a low-risk, low-annual return strategy like the one in Table 12.1. A 25-year-old earning $30,000, just starting out by investing a modest 5 percent of his annual income in his company's 401(k) plan, stands to enjoy an 11.86 percent annual rate of return. In the 40 years until his retirement at age 65, that asset allocation portfolio would grow to an estimated $2.99 million.

Figure 12.1 and the table that follows show how switching from a low-risk to a high-risk asset allocation could lift this investor's return to 13.36 percent, leading to a robust $4.6 million nest egg.

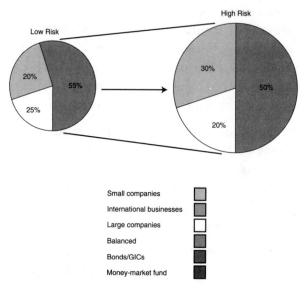

Small companies

International businesses

Large companies

Balanced

Bonds/GICs

Money-market fund

Figure 12.1 This 25-year-old employee could add more than $1.6 million to his or her nest egg by switching from a conservative to an aggressive asset allocation. But can the employee tolerate the additional risk?

ASSET ALLOCATION	LOW RISK	HIGH RISK
Small companies:	20%	50%
International businesses:	25%	30%
Large companies:	55%	20%
Balanced:		
Bonds/GICs:		
Money-market fund:		
Estimated annual rate of return:	11.86%	13.36%
Estimated account value at retirement:	$2,997,700	$4,651,700

A 45-year-old employee, earning $60,000, with a 401(k) account already worth $55,000 through low-risk investments of 7 percent of his or her income, could end up with more than $1 million if he sticks with the conservative strategy. A moderate-risk allocation will boost his retirement-age nest egg by $240,200. A high-risk strategy is likely to provide him with savings of $1.5 million by age 65.

If this employee switches to an aggressive asset allocation, Figure 12.2 and the table that follows illustrate the different asset allocation achieved by switching to a high-risk strategy, and the greater account value that could result.

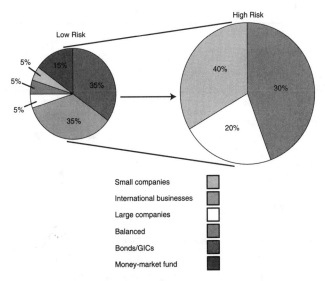

Figure 12.2 By switching from a low-risk to a high-risk asset allocation, a 45-year-old worker who contributes 7% of his or her $60,000 annual income to a 401(k) plan could boost the size of his or her nest egg by nearly 50%. Would the added risk be worth it to you?

ASSET ALLOCATION	LOW RISK	HIGH RISK
Small companies:	5%	40%
International businesses:	5%	30%
Large companies:	5%	20%
Balanced:	35%	10%
Bonds/GICs:	35%	
Money-market fund:	15%	
Estimated annual rate of return:	10.56%	13.09%
Estimated account value at retirement:	$1,010,100	$1,508,400

Similar differences result at any age. The more risk you are willing to assume, the higher your reward is likely to be.

In this lesson, you learned how to translate your level of risk-tolerance into a practical investment strategy. In the next lesson, you will learn a comprehensive set of investment guidelines.

ACKNOWLEDGMENTS

Contributions to asset allocation modeling: David England, Waddell & Reed, Brookline, MA; Thomas Fee, Third Party Educational Systems; Dee Lee, Harvard Financial Educators; Catherine Friend White, Financial Architects, Lexington, MA.

Computer projections of asset allocation models: MasteryPOINT 401(k) program by Third Party Educational Systems, Minn., MN.

* Source: ©*Stocks, Bonds, Bills, and Inflation 1995 Yearbook*™, Ibbotson Associates, Chicago, IL (annually updates work by Roger G. Ibbotson and Rex A. Sinquefield). Used by permission. All rights reserved.

13

SELECTING INVESTMENTS

In this lesson, you will learn a comprehensive set of investment guidelines.

Selecting investments that are right for you will depend on a large number of variables, such as your risk tolerance. You must also ask several things about every investment option, starting with: How well does it perform? (See Lesson 15.)

No matter what individual variables you must consider, there are seven rules you should follow because they apply to everyone in a 401(k) plan.

SEVEN GUIDELINES

Some of these rules come from earlier lessons. Others are new concepts. Together, they form a comprehensive set of investment guidelines.

1. DON'T DELAY

Do not postpone investing until you "think you can afford it." Saving and investing do not get easier as you get older; as your income increases, so do your expenses and obligations.

If you still feel unable to invest as much of your income as Line 9 in our worksheet in Lesson 6 indicated you should, start with less and gradually increase that amount each year.

2. DIVERSIFY

As you learned in earlier lessons, you can reduce your investment risks by diversifying. Unless you intentionally want to take risks in pursuit of possible higher returns, you should not invest in funds that do the opposite of diversifying by confining their investments to specialized categories.

Those categories include: individual nations or geographic areas, industrial sectors, types of commodities (like gold), or even concepts (like so-called socially screened funds that invest only in businesses that follow a list of social or political do's and don'ts).

3. INVEST FOR GROWTH

As a general rule, you want your 401(k) nest egg to grow large by the time you retire, so it can generate as much income as possible for you to live on.

One key to growth is beating the rate of inflation by as much as you can. History has shown that you are more likely to accomplish that over time with stocks and stock-based mutual funds than with fixed-income investments like bonds and bond-based funds or cash-equivalents.

Accordingly, the time to favor growth-oriented investments is while you're young and can afford to let your nest egg grow rather than generate income to live on.

4. INVEST LONG TERM

This means ignoring short-term swings in the market, sticking with your asset-allocation strategy, and giving your account time to grow.

It also means figuring how much money you'll need for upcoming expenses and emergencies, and setting aside money in something like a money market account to pay for those.

That way, you won't have to raise money by selling shares of stock or a mutual fund when the market is down, losing part of the money you originally contributed.

5. DON'T CONFUSE "SAFETY" WITH "PREDICTABILITY"

Don't make a mistake that many inexperienced investors do: Do not confuse "safety" with "predictability."

Many inexperienced investors believe fixed-income investments are "safer" than stock-based investments because they generate income in a predictable way. But if safety means staying as far ahead of inflation as possible and cultivating a nest egg that's as large as possible, then fixed-income investments are not safe—at least, not as safe as stock-based investments.

6. AVOID NEW MUTUAL FUNDS AND MANAGERS

You should study prospectuses and other information to select investments that seem likely to perform well in the future because they have performed well repeatedly in the past. Even then, past performance is no guarantee of future success.

A new mutual fund, or a fund with an unproven manager, then, probably cannot provide any evidence that it is likely to perform well in the future. It has no track record.

Information about a fund manager is in the fund's prospectus. The fund itself will also provide information.

7. ASSET-ALLOCATION ADJUSTMENTS

From time to time you will need to change your contributions to your account to keep your mix of investments in line with your asset-allocation strategy. That's because your strategy will shift as your age and circumstances change. You'll also want to change if one (or more) investment performs so much better or worse than your others that it becomes a larger or smaller share of your overall account than you want.

However, you should resist doing this after big swings in the stock market. Those changes are temporary, and you should think *long-term* with your investments.

Realign your investments generally no more than once a year. The best way to realign is by increasing contributions into funds that have shrunk below their intended share of your account, becoming relatively less expensive.

You should not rebalance by pulling money out of funds that have grown. However, if a fund under-performs for two or three years, consider switching to a better one in that asset category.

In this lesson you learned a comprehensive set of investment guidelines. In the next lesson you will learn the first of several steps in fine-tuning your account.

14

Understanding Your Own 401(k) Plan Account

In this lesson, you will learn what information is available and how to get it so you can periodically check up on your account.

First, Understand the National Ground Rules

In the past few lessons you learned how to select investments for your 401(k) account.

Periodically, though, you need to check up on your account. You will want to know how your investments are doing. You also need to confirm that your account record is free of errors and that you are being credited for all your contributions and earnings.

In addition, you need to make sure that your asset allocation is what you want. As time passes, earnings may gradually enlarge your holdings in one or more investments, upsetting the diversification ratio that you selected as a result of your level of risk tolerance. Likewise, over time, your asset allocation strategy is likely to change simply because your age and circumstances have too.

Thus, you will have several reasons to look in on your account: curiosity, safety check, periodic fine-tuning. This may be very simple. Your plan may offer you few choices, which reduces the amount of information available:

- Your company plan is allowed to offer only a single investment option. Only a very small percentage of company plans do that, however.

- It is also allowed to offer a small number of options on an all-or-nothing basis—either you invest in all of them, or none of them.

- Your company is allowed to limit how much money you invest.

- Your company is allowed to limit how much money you put into a particular investment.

- Your company is allowed to select how it invests its matching contribution—without consulting you.

However, the majority of companies offer more options and choices.

TWO SETS OF RULES

The reason some companies offer you few choices and others offer you many is that companies are given two sets of federal rules to follow. The older set contains the basic guidelines for a 401(k) plan; it makes fewer demands on companies. The newer rules, with more current updates, establish tougher guidelines. In addition, competitive pressures also motivate your company to reveal more than it has to.

That second set of government rules is known as the *404(c) regulations*. Your company can give you the control that is called for by Section 404(c) by complying with the standards that section of the Employment Retirement Income Security Act (ERISA) establishes. Many company plans, even if they are not officially seeking status as 404(c) plans, play it safe by trying to meet the 404(c) standards to protect themselves from future legal blame for 401(k) investments performing below expectations.

404(c) Rules   The number refers to the section of ERISA, which is a federal law that sets minimum standards for pension plans in private industry. Basically, section 404(c) says if your company gives you "control" over your 401(k) investments, the government will excuse your company from liability for any losses you suffer with your 401(k) account.

In either case, because they are only minimum standards, companies may exceed them and do more for you than the law requires. That leeway is one reason plans differ so much from each other.

To get a feel for how easy it will be to obtain information about your account, find out whether your company's plan complies with section 404(c). To find out, just ask your Plan Administrator or a company benefits counselor. Your company must inform you whether the plan complies with 404(c).

Even without 404(c), your company is required to tell you how your account overall is doing: a lump-sum valuation of your entire account. Your company will do this in the document called the Individual Benefit Statement, which, as you learned in Lesson 4, your company must provide to you once a year.

NEXT, LEARN YOUR COMPANY'S RULES

Most employers will provide you with more than the minimum required by law. In fact, it is estimated that more than nine out of 10 companies follow at least some 404(c) rules even if they have not officially adopted that section of ERISA.*

In contrast to the basic requirements, those 404(c) rules require your company to do many things for you.

- You must be given "control" over your investments and you must be given enough information to make "informed" investment decisions.

- Your company must give you at least three investment choices, each of which is different enough from the others that it provides different risk and return characteristics. The idea is to offer you a choice among investments that are designed not to suffer losses at the same time.

 Giving You Real Choices Your company is required to offer you investments as different as a money market fund, a stock fund, and a bond fund.

- At least once every three months—four times a year—you must have a chance to change your investments as well as how much you invest.

Those are the most important "how-to" information rules that work in your favor.

YOUR RIGHT TO OTHER IMPORTANT INFORMATION

Your company's plan is also required to give you other important information to enable you to control your account through informed decisions.

What federal regulations do not specify, however, is *how* your company must provide this information. To encourage companies to offer 401(k) plans, the law lets each company choose its own manner of distributing information. Some companies leave it to an outside investment manager; some companies produce their own literature and videotapes; some distribute documents provided by mutual funds that are among their plans' investment choices; some include detailed information in their Summary Plan Description (SPD).

There are no rules about how or where you will find information. The rules only specify that—*somehow*—you receive the following, even if you do not ask for it:

- A description of each investment option, including each one's investment goals and risk-and-return characteristics.

- Information, including identity and location, of your plan's investment manager. (You can find this in your SPD.)

- An explanation of what process you follow to make your investments.

- A description of any transaction fees and expenses that may be charged to your account when you change investments or buy and sell investments. These fees and expenses may be called *commissions*, *sales loads*, *deferred sales charges*, and *redemption* or *exchange fees*.

- A copy of the *prospectus* for each mutual fund in which you have invested, if you haven't already been provided with a fund's prospectus before investing.

Prospectus   A brochure that contains information about a stock, bond, or mutual fund, which describes key information such as the fund's performance history, manager(s), goals, and finances.

- An explanation of your rights as a shareholder in any company or mutual fund whose stock you buy. For example, you may have shareholder voting rights.

In addition, your company's plan is required to give you, if you request it:

- Copies of any financial statements, reports, or other material relating to your investment options, which if provided to your plan must be made available to you.

- A list of the assets owned by each investment option. For example, this would include a list of the stocks or bonds in which a mutual fund invests. This information is in a mutual fund prospectus, but if your plan acquires updated information it must provide it to you upon request.

- Information concerning the value of shares, or *units*, in investment options available to you.

- Information concerning the value of shares or units in the investments you actually own in your account.

You may be able to supplement those sources of information with one other source of information:

- Mutual funds are required twice a year to disclose what stocks, bonds, and other assets they have invested in. They send this information to shareholders. You may receive it directly. Some mutual funds take a legalistic approach and consider the plan, not you, to be the investor; they send reports to the plan, from which you are allowed to obtain the information. Your plan may provide it without your asking.

On the other hand, there is information that you may not expect to receive. Before anyone sells you a publicly traded security, they are required by federal law to provide you with a prospectus. However, some mutual funds offered by your plan may not be publicly traded, so they are exempt from that requirement. Such funds are sometimes called *pooled* investments, which may be insurance products or mutual funds sold only to certain people, like participants in your 401(k) plan, and not to the general public. Although you may not be able to obtain a prospectus for such funds, you should ask the plan administrator or a company benefits counselor for all the information he or she has.

MORE WAYS TO LEARN WHAT YOU NEED

To learn about your 401(k) plan overall and your account in particular, you should start by:

- Reading your company's Summary Plan Description.

- Asking your Plan Administrator or a company benefits adviser what other information is available from your plan or its mutual funds.

In addition, your company may be one of the growing number using innovative ways to inform workers about their 401(k) plans and their accounts. Two of the most important of those are:

- Video and audio tapes—if your company provides them, take advantage.

- Seminars offered by your company's plan—they can be an excellent way to learn and ask questions about your plan and your investment choices. They are also a convenient way to meet someone connected to your plan who can give you information on a regular basis.

OUTSIDE SOURCES OF INFORMATION

You can also learn about your individual investment options from the many daily, weekly, and monthly news publications distributing information about stocks, bonds, mutual funds, and other types of investments. Four times a year (around the end of each business quarter), many publications produce helpful and detailed tables showing how mutual funds have performed during that quarter and recent time intervals such as the past month, six months, year, and various multi-year periods. These publications are available at libraries, on newsstands, and by subscription.

Also, you can get custom-tailored advice from a professional financial planner.

Specializing in Mutual Funds

Two other resources specialize in mutual funds. Since most of your 401(k) investment choices are mutual funds, you should know about these—they're comprehensive, easy-to-find, and easy-to-use:

Morningstar Mutual Funds (800-876-5005) and *Value Line's Mutual Fund Survey* (800-284-7607) are notebook publications that are updated frequently and regularly with insertable pages. Both provide information about well over 1,000 mutual funds, describing their returns, risks, and expenses. They have become standard reference sources for investors. They are available at many libraries, from some brokers, and as subscriptions.

In this lesson, you learned how to get information about your account so you can adjust your account to match your needs. In the next lesson, you will learn an important way to evaluate the performance of a mutual fund.

Acknowledgments

*Source: KPMG Peat Marwick.

*Contributions to interpretation of disclosure regulations: U.S. Dept. of Labor and David Wray, Profit Sharing/401(k) Council of America.

Judging Mutual Fund Performance

In this lesson, you will learn about total return, one of the most important measurements of a mutual fund's performance and value.

Because most of your 401(k) investment choices are likely to be mutual funds, it is important for you to learn how to judge their potential value as investments. Although past performance is never a guarantee of future results, how a fund has done previously remains one of the best guides to how well it's likely to do in the future.

In turn, one of the most important yardsticks of a fund's performance is its total return.

As you learned in Lesson 6, total return means how much you earn or lose on your mutual fund investment, measured by the fund's price-per-share increase or decrease plus its income from dividends or *capital gains* (profits from the sale of stock or bonds by the fund manager), which the fund passes along to its own shareholders. If your mutual fund's price per share rises from $10 to $15 and it pays you a dividend of 10 cents per share, your total return is $5.10 or 51 percent.

Other Measurements You should not confuse total return with other important measurements such as **yield**. Yield generally refers to payments like interest or dividends. For example, if a stock or mutual fund whose price per share is $10 pays $1 a year in dividends, its yield is 10 percent. However, unlike total return, that doesn't take into account any change in the share price itself.

How To Use Total Return

Here's how to use total return to assess a fund's future prospects: Look at its average annual total return over the most recent five-year period. That's more important than its total return in the most recent one-year period. You want to learn how consistent and reliable a fund is, not whether it had a single good or bad year, which may not be typical of how it usually performs.

Next, if you have a choice of several funds in each asset-allocation group, such as large-company stocks or intermediate government bonds, focus on the ones whose total returns over five years have been in the top 20 or 25 percent of their category.

Where You Can Find This Information

There are several ways you can find out how well a mutual fund has performed during various periods of time and how well its performance compares to similar funds.

- A mutual fund's prospectus typically reports the fund's total return in each recent year. Look for a table of "financial highlights" near the front of the prospectus. If this information is not in the prospectus, it will be in the fund's annual report.

- A mutual fund's annual and semiannual report generally lists the fund's average annual total return during periods of time such as one, three, five, or 10 years in a section titled "Performance." The list also compares the fund's average annual total return in those periods to yardsticks such as the Standard & Poor's index of 500 stocks (which is a popular mirror of the whole stock market's performance because it tracks the performance of 500 large and mid-size companies). In addition, such lists often compare the fund's performance to similar funds in its category (such as "sector," "growth," or "small-company"). The list may contain other benchmarks as well, such as the Consumer Price Index (a measurement of consumer prices and inflation).

- Those performance numbers are illustrated in a chart that illustrates how a hypothetical $10,000 would have grown over a number of years if you had invested it in the mutual fund or in some comparable index (like the Standard & Poor 500). This is usually in the annual and semiannual reports.

- If you can't find the annual report information described above, look in the prospectus. It must be in one or the other.

- Personal-finance magazines and newspaper business sections also periodically list mutual funds' total returns, both for various time periods and in comparison to similar groups of funds and other investments. Your local librarian may also have specialty publications that contain this information.

TWO LAST POINTS

Regardless of where you find the information, remember that another reason you should measure performance over time, rather than simply the most recent single year, is that investing long-term is one of your best defenses against risk.

Finally, once you identify the best-performing funds in the categories or groups you want, you can further narrow down your choices by seeing which ones will cost you less.

In this lesson, you learned how to judge a mutual fund's performance and potential as an investment by its total return. In the next lesson, you learn how to understand how much a fund costs you.

YOUR MUTUAL FUND EXPENSES

16

In this lesson, you will learn about the costs and fees charged by mutual funds.

Since most of your investment choices are likely to be mutual funds, understanding how much a mutual fund costs will help you choose your investments for several reasons:

- There are a variety of fees and expenses, such as operating expenses, sales charges, and your individual plan's fees.

- Those fees and expenses vary. Some mutual funds may not charge you any fee to invest, while others will charge you a fee of 5.5 percent or more. Some charge you when you buy shares, others when you sell. These fees vary significantly.

- You may have to pay other expenses as well, such as a fee to a broker or financial adviser who helps you buy shares.

COSTS VARY AMONG FUNDS

Funds may impose sales charges or operating expenses that are dramatically different—several percentage points apart. On the other hand, cost differences may be mere fractions of a percentage point, but those costs still matter because they add up over the years.

All other things (such as a fund's investment performance and its manager's track record) being relatively equal, cost may be the deciding factor in determining which fund offers you the better potential return.

High costs also drive up risk, because a fund manager will take more chances to improve his or her fund's performance to make up the difference.

Costs may not only help you choose between mutual funds; costs may also help you select from investment options that are different, but have similarities that may disguise those differences. For example, a Guaranteed Investment Contract (GIC) issued by an insurance company may pay a similar return to a fixed-income mutual fund, but the GIC may cost you more because insurers often impose higher investment fees than fund companies.

A VARIETY OF FEES AND EXPENSES

Like total return, you can determine fees and expenses through numerous sources, including a fund's prospectus. There are different types of fees and expenses.

OPERATING EXPENSES

The most useful figure for mutual funds is the *expense ratio*, which tells you how much the fund is charging you each year to pay for operating expenses. The figure is expressed as a percentage of the fund's assets, and usually ranges between 1 and 1.5 percent. (The average for a typical stock fund is 1.4 percent.) The lower the expense ratio, the better.

You can find the expense ratio in a prospectus. In the same section you will see the annual operating expenses translated into a dollar amount. In a table, it will show how much your expenses would be on a hypothetical $1,000 investment in that fund, if the fund earned 5 percent annually, after such intervals as one, three, five, and 10 years.

12b-1 fee   An annual operating expense charged by mutual funds; it's simply a marketing fee: you are charged for the fund's advertising. Like many fees, it is taken from your fund's assets. The charge may range as high as 1 percent of a fund's assets. Such fees are often imposed by mutual funds that call themselves *no-load* (which means you are not assessed a fee when you buy or sell shares), but which then assess 12b-1 fees—one reason these fees are often criticized. A 12b-1 fee under 0.4 percent annually is considered more acceptable.

SALES CHARGES

When you buy or sell shares, mutual funds often assess a charge, which is called a *load*. There are three types:

Front-end load (or **front load**)   This is a sales charge you pay when you purchase shares in a mutual fund. It is a percentage of the amount you invest. For example, a 3 percent front load means you pay 3 percent of the amount you invest as a sales commission to the fund or broker. It is often simply subtracted from the amount you invest, so a 3 percent front load on a $1,000 investment would mean you are credited with buying $970 worth of shares, with $30 subtracted as the sales charge.

Some funds charge on a sliding scale, so if you buy or sell more than a designated amount of shares you pay a lower rate.

Back-end load (also known as a **back load** or **deferred sales charge**)   A sales charge you pay when you sell shares. It is calculated on the value of the shares you sell. For example, a back-end load of 3 percent on $5,000 worth of shares is $150.

No-load   Many mutual funds do not charge any fee for buying or selling shares. Many investors think of loads as sales commissions paid for investment advice.

If you make your own investment decisions without help from a broker, financial planner, or some other adviser, you may prefer to choose no-load (or *low-load*—see below) funds.

Likewise, if your plan offers a small number of investment options, your choices may be easy. Ask yourself whether you receive enough service or advice to justify a high load. Similarly, decide whether the fund's total return—especially in comparison to your other choices—makes up the difference for a high load.

Funds that charge *low loads* (usually 3 percent or less) are often categorized as no-loads. Be sure you understand whether a "no-load" fund in fact charges a load.

Deceptive costs   Some investment advisers offer so-called "class B" or "class C" shares of a mutual fund. Instead of a single front load, such funds may charge a lower-number fee or load annually. The fund may be promoted as a low load or even a no-load, costing less than a front-load fund. But if the smaller percentage load is charged year after year it may end up costing you more.

Always ask the person selling you fund shares to explain all costs, whether they are called fees, expenses, loads, commissions, or charges.

YOUR PLAN'S FEES

Your company may pay for some or all of your plan's administrative costs. However, companies are increasingly shifting such costs to you and other participants. You may be charged anywhere from about $20 to $150 for such "administrative" fees.

OTHER EXPENSES

A small percentage of 401(k) plans permit you to make investments on your own, without being restricted to a choice of funds, stocks, or other investment assets offered by the plan. If you are in one of these plans, you may have to pay fees to a stockbroker or financial planner outside your plan. These fees may be commissions on each transaction or flat annual fees.

In either case, you may try to negotiate the fees down.

In this lesson, you learned how to understand your mutual fund costs. In the next lesson, you will learn how to determine the amount you may contribute each year to your account.

17

CONTRIBUTING TO YOUR ACCOUNT

In this lesson, you will learn how to determine the maximum amount you are allowed to contribute each year to your 401(k) plan.

HOW MUCH ARE YOU ALLOWED TO CONTRIBUTE TO YOUR ACCOUNT?

The maximum amount you're allowed to contribute to your 401(k) plan account is determined by five restrictions. Three of them are set by the government:

1. The Internal Revenue Service sets a dollar limit, which for tax year 1996 is $9,500. If the cost-of-living rises by more than a certain amount, the IRS adjusts that annual cap. $9,500 is the limit on *your* contribution, not on any matching contribution from your employer.

2. The Internal Revenue code also limits the combined total amount that can be put into your 401(k) plan as well as any other *defined contribution* retirement plans you have, including a profit-sharing plan if

you participate in one at work. In addition, the total amount includes not only your contributions but contributions your employer makes too. The limit set by the IRS is 25 percent of your taxable income or $30,000—whichever is less.

This second rule is in addition to, not instead of, the primary restriction of $9,500. If you don't have any other defined-contribution plan or any employer contributions, it does not mean you may raise your limit to $30,000.

3. The government puts additional limits on how much you are allowed to contribute if you are, by certain federal definitions, a highly paid employee. What the government does is limit the size of the gap between how much highly paid workers and lower-paid workers contribute. This restriction is calculated on a percentage basis rather than a dollar-amount basis.

If you happen to be a *highly compensated employee* (HCE), your company is responsible for making the complicated calculation. If the HCEs as a group exceed their limit, they actually may have to give back the money! If that happens and you are an HCE, your employer will send you a check for the excess amount. Of course, since it is no longer tax-deferred, you have to pay taxes on it.

(If your company closes the gap by making a special contribution to NHCEs' 401(k) accounts, the HCEs may not have to give back their money.)

Why This Rule Exists   The idea is to prevent a company from offering a better deal to the highest paid employees than to rank-and-file workers. The rule encourages companies to make sure large numbers of employees benefit from their 401(k) plans.

ARE YOU "HIGHLY PAID"?

The definition of highly compensated employee (HCE) applies to a lot of ordinary managers, executives, and other workers—possibly including you—not just the top corporate executives. Two ways you may fit the definition are

- You earn at least $66,000 and are among the 20 percent highest paid people in your company; or

- You earn $100,000 or more annually, regardless of standing. (Both dollar amounts will rise over the years because they're tied to the rate of inflation.)

TWO OTHER RESTRICTIONS

In addition to the governmental restrictions, your employer may restrict the amount you contribute yearly and you may limit your own contribution.

VOLUNTARY LIMITS: THE LESS, THE BETTER

Within all the other limits, this one is entirely under your control. You may limit yourself according to the demands made on your paycheck by such things as your living expenses and personal circumstances.

Two things that should not limit your contribution are uncertainty and low risk tolerance. This book has taught you how your 401(k) works, how to decide how large of a retirement nest egg to aim for, and how to invest your way towards that goal. The worst thing you can do is to do nothing. As for fear about investing, this book has also taught you how to honestly measure how much riskiness you can put up with in your investments, and how to select investments that match your tolerance for volatility.

As you have learned, the general rule is, the less you limit yourself, the more you'll end up with. The more you save and invest, the larger your retirement nest egg will become.

RESTRICTIONS SET BY YOUR COMPANY

In addition to contribution limits set by the government, companies may set their own limits, often to reduce administrative burdens. Your company is allowed to restrict your annual contribution to any amount less than the $9,500. However, your company is not allowed to set the limit higher.

Your employer is also allowed to establish a minimum level. Most companies require you to contribute at least 1 or 2 percent of your pay. Generally, companies allow you to contribute anywhere from 1 percent to 15 percent of your pay, with 14 percent being the average ceiling.

The amount workers actually contribute is far below that, however. Only one out of every 20 workers contributes the maximum. Your fellow workers contribute an average of only 5 percent of their pay—because of the government's limitation rules and because they believe they cannot afford more.

DON'T HANDICAP YOURSELF

You should avoid adding unnecessarily to the restrictions set by your company and the government:

You can afford it   When deciding how much you will contribute (after figuring out how much you should contribute), try not to limit yourself. Your contributions are done automatically through your company's payroll department; you do not have to write a check or hand over cash. Your contribution is money you never see, which is easier than having to dig money out of your checking account, wallet, or purse.

Aim high   If you decide to contribute 10 percent of your pay to your account but you want to work your way up to that amount to make sure you can live without it, don't start too low. Start as high as you dare, because every dollar you do contribute will grow over the years for you. Don't deprive yourself.

In this lesson, you learned how to determine the maximum amount you are allowed to contribute each year to your 401(k) plan account. In the next lesson, you will learn about contributions your company can make to your account and about extra contributions you may be eligible to make.

ACKNOWLEDGMENTS

Contributions to analysis of rules concerning highly compensated employees: Robert Liberto, vice president of The Segal Co.

Statistics regarding employee contribution levels: KPMG Peat Marwick.

18

ADDITIONAL CONTRIBUTIONS TO YOUR ACCOUNT

In this lesson, you will learn how both you and your employer may be able to make additional contributions to your 401(k) plan account.

A KEY BENEFIT OF 401(K) PLANS

In addition to your own contribution, your company is allowed to contribute to your account. This is among the most important features of your company's 401(k) plan.

It is known as a *matching contribution* because your company matches what you contribute. Here are key things you should know about it:

- Usually your company does not match your entire contribution. Your company is allowed to decide how much of your contribution it will match.

- Your company is also allowed to decide what form its matching contribution will take. Almost all companies contribute either cash (which you can invest), company stock, or some combination of the two.

- Your company is even allowed to offer its match only if you meet a certain condition, like investing in a particular option offered by the plan. Typically, company stock is what you have to invest in to earn the matching contribution.

Like many of the benefits available in your company's 401(k) plan, the matching contribution is a voluntary feature. Your company is not required to contribute to your account. But, your company probably does; 84 out of every 100 companies do.

RECOGNIZING A GOOD THING

The odds that you will be motivated to participate in your company's 401(k) plan increase dramatically if your company offers a matching contribution. Barely four out of 10 workers bother to enroll in plans that do not offer an employer match. In contrast, workers flock to plans that do offer a match. About two out of every three workers enroll in plans with an employer-match feature.

The reason companies offer 401(k) plans and that employees like them is simple: they are equivalent to a pay raise, and both the money itself and what it earns are tax-deferred. If you don't participate in your company's 401(k) plan, not only are you depriving yourself of a way to save and earn money for retirement; you are also giving up a pay raise.

For a company, a 401(k) plan with an employer match is a good way to attract and keep good workers. The most common employer match is 50 percent. That means your company will match half of what you contribute to your account. The next most common match is 25 percent, with 100 percent matches trailing that.

UNCLEAR INCENTIVE

You are more likely to participate in your company's 401(k) plan the higher your company's matching contribution is—but only to a limited extent. Employee participation rates rise as the employer's match increases:

> Only 41 percent of employees participate where there is no match.

> 55 percent participate in plans that offer 10 cents for every employee dollar.

> 57 percent participate in plans that offer 25 cents.

> 64 percent participate in plans that offer 50 cents.

> 70 percent participate in plans that offer 75 cents.

But participation declines to 66 percent in plans that offer one dollar. Some companies may not provide sufficient information for employees to understand plans that offer many options or complicated options. If you decline to participate in your company's plan because the match seems low, you are misinterpreting the value of the matching contribution. For instance, if your company contributes 25 cents for every $1 you do, you should not think of those 25 cents as merely one-quarter the amount you are investing. Think of it as a guaranteed 25 percent return on your dollar.

That is about five times better than what your money would earn in a savings bank account. And that's before your dollar starts to earn any investment return. In addition, it is before the company's 25 percent contribution starts to earn a return as well. Moreover, all of that money will grow by compounding through time.

In any case, companies almost always limit their match. No matter how much a company contributes as its match, most companies limit their match to the first 6 to 7 percent of an employee's pay. In such a plan, if you contribute 15 percent of your pay to your account, you will receive a match on less than half what you contribute.

That's the case whatever amount a company match consists of—anywhere from pennies up to dollar-for-dollar. And the cap may be lower. For example, 12 percent of companies limit their match to the first 3 percent.

Companies may also grant their match in steps. For example, your company may match your contribution on the first 4 percent of your pay dollar-for-dollar. But the next 2 percent of your pay may be matched only 50 cents to the dollar, and the amount beyond the first 6 percent may not receive any match.

A small proportion of companies impose a dollar limit, as opposed to a percentage limit. When companies do, the average limit is $750.

In any event, you should neither decline to participate nor limit your participation because of the size, number, or complexity of your company's matching contribution rules. This lesson will help you sort through those rules so you can take advantage of the company-match feature. Any amount you receive is like a raise, bonus, or boost to the total return earned by your own money. If you do not take advantage of it, you are cutting your own pay and investment performance.

Important Detail   One of the most important aspects of your company's matching contribution is that you may not own it right away. In sharp contrast, you own your own contributions from the start. Your company may require that you work there a certain amount of time in order to own (or become *vested* in) the company's matching contribution. You can read more about this in Lesson 20.

AFTER-TAX CONTRIBUTIONS

You may be among the four out of every 10 workers to be enrolled in a 401(k) plan that permits you to make *after-tax* contributions to your account.

That's different from the way you usually contribute to your 401(k) account, which is with before-tax money. From earlier lessons, you'll recall that the before-tax contribution is one of the principle benefits of a 401(k) plan. A before-tax contribution is money you invest without paying current income taxes on it. Once you invest it, you're also excused from paying taxes on whatever it earns year by year. (You only pay taxes when you withdraw the money—presumably after retirement.)

In contrast, after-tax money is counted as part of your pay for tax purposes. You pay income taxes on it along with the rest of your pay.

The advantage of an after-tax contribution, however, is that its *earnings* are tax-deferred, just like your regular (before-tax) 401(k) contributions. Year after year that money grows, without taxes whittling away at it. That enables it to grow more than if you had invested it outside of your 401(k) plan altogether.

Another similarity to your before-tax contributions is that your company may limit how much you're allowed to invest this way. Whereas the typical company will permit you to invest up to 14 percent of your before-tax income, the typical company will permit you to invest 13 percent of your after-tax pay.

A third similarity to before-tax contributions is that your company may make a matching contribution, but not many companies do.

Taxing Differences   After- and before-tax contributions have important similarities and differences when it comes to tax consequences.

One difference is that, before or after retirement, you can usually withdraw after-tax contributions, for any reason, without paying income taxes—because you've already paid those taxes! (Early withdrawals of before-tax contributions are permitted only for certain purposes.)

A similarity between the two categories of contributions is that when you withdraw money you earn on after-tax contributions, that will be subject to income taxes and an early-withdrawal penalty of 10 percent under certain circumstances, like if you are younger than 59 1/2.

That 10 percent penalty may be a good reason not to put money into your 401(k) account that you expect to withdraw before retirement age. However, it could be worthwhile to do that anyway if, together with your employer's matching contribution, your after-tax contributions still earn a desirable rate of return even after subtracting the penalty.

In this lesson, you learned how you and your employer may be allowed to make additional contributions to your 401(k) plan account. In the next lesson, you will learn when and how you gain ownership of your company's matching contribution to your account.

ACKNOWLEDGMENTS

Statistics regarding participation rates, matching contributions, and after-tax contributions: KPMG Peat Marwick.

19

VESTING

In this lesson, you learn about vesting.

You own 100 percent of your own contributions and their investment earnings at all times. That is true whether the money is invested as a before- or after-tax contribution. If you leave your company, you are entitled to take all of that with you.

In addition, your company may give you full ownership of its matching contribution as soon as you enroll in your company's plan. However, your company is not required to.

Instead, your company may require that you gain gradual ownership of its matching contribution (or of any other contribution your company may make to your account). The *vesting* process refers to the amount of time you must work for your company to gain 100 percent ownership.

Accrued Benefits The amount of benefit that has accumulated or been allocated in your name in your 401(k) plan (and in any other pension plan you may participate in) as of a specific time. In the case of your 401(k) plan, it refers to all of your own contributions as well as any contributions made by your company, whether or not you are fully vested in them.

WHEN YOU BECOME VESTED

Generally, there are three rules defining when you become vested:

Rule Number One: Your company must follow a schedule that vests you at least as quickly as one of these two timetables:

- You must be 100 percent vested after five years of service.

- You must be vested gradually in steps over seven years. You become 20 percent vested (that is, you own 20 percent or one-fifth) after three years of service, and 20 percent more each year until you are 100 percent vested after seven years.

In contrast to a seven-year schedule that builds your ownership in gradual steps (see Table 19.2), five-year schedules are nicknamed "cliff" schedules because your ownership rises from zero to 100 percent in a single step, like a cliff rising abruptly from a flat landscape (see Table 19.1).

TABLE 19.1   FIVE-YEAR "CLIFF" VESTING SCHEDULE

YEARS YOU HAVE WORKED FOR YOUR COMPANY	PERCENTAGE OF EMPLOYER'S CONTRIBUTIONS THAT YOU OWN
Less than 5	0%
At least 5	100%

Source: U.S. Dept. of Labor

Table 19.2   Continued

Years you have worked for your company	Percentage of employer's contributions that you own
Less than 3	0 %
3 (but less than 4)	20%
4 (but less than 5)	40%
5 (but less than 6)	60%
6 (but less than 7)	80%
7 (but less than 8)	100%

Source: U.S. Dept. of Labor

Rule Number Two: You become vested when you reach your company plan's normal retirement age even if it is less than your company's vesting schedule calls for. For example, if your company's normal retirement age is 65 and you reach that after three years of service, you are vested at that point even if your company has a five-year vesting schedule.

Rule Number Three: If your company plan's vesting schedule is changed after you have been employed there at least three years, you have the right to select the vesting schedule that existed before the change. You would want to do that if the earlier vesting schedule was faster.

How Vesting Helps You

The two most important things about vesting are these: You own and can take with you whatever percentage of your company's contributions are vested. Similarly, you may forfeit whatever part of your company's contributions are not vested if you leave your company.

To illustrate, assume these hypothetical facts: Your company has a seven-year vesting schedule. Your annual contribution is $2,000 and your company's match is $1,000 a year. You have worked there four years and you have been a member of the plan since the start of your employment. You would have contributed $8,000 and your company has contributed $4,000.

If you leave the company, you would be entitled to all of your own contribution of $8,000 (plus whatever it has earned) and 40 percent—or $1,600—of your company's $4,000 contribution as well as 40 percent of whatever it has earned.

ADDITIONAL RULES

There are a number of additional rules concerning vesting. Most permit or even require your employer to vest you more quickly than the minimum timetables discussed above. However, some special rules spell out when your employer may limit your vesting benefit.

The law requires that a company's vesting schedule be at least as fast as the five-year and seven-year timetables. That means your company may adopt a *cliff* schedule that makes you 100 percent vested in less than five years. If your company adopts a *graded* schedule, it may create one that vests you sooner than seven years or gives you bigger ownership steps along the way than the standard timetable.

Generally, all of your years of employment at your company count towards your vesting in that company's plan, including any years you worked there before participating in the plan.

However, under certain circumstances your company may disregard some of your time of employment for vesting purposes. Those circumstances must be spelled out in the plan's rules and regulations, which you can find in your Summary

Plan Description (see Lesson 4). If, for example, a plan uses a more generous vesting schedule than the law requires, you may have to forfeit the extra benefits you gain if you are terminated for dishonesty.

If you leave your company (even if you are fired), you may be able to leave your 401(k) account behind and allow it to continue to grow (although you will not be able to make new contributions or receive any more company matching funds).

However, if the vested amount in your account is less than $3,500, your company may require that you withdraw it. In that case, you would get to choose how to take that distribution. You may decide to transfer it to your 401(k) plan account in your new workplace or to a rollover Individual Retirement Account (IRA).

Avoid Tax Penalties   Even if you are required to withdraw your account money, the choice of how to take that distribution remains up to you. To avoid the very expensive tax penalty that you learned about in Lesson 5, you should never allow direct payment of the money to you.

If you work for a company whose plan is especially generous to workers known as *key employees*, special rules apply. The plan must provide faster vesting than the standard five- or seven-year schedules. A timetable at least as fast as one of the following two must be used:

> If your company wants to adopt a "cliff" schedule, instead of a five-year schedule it must make you 100 percent vested in no more than three years.

If your company wants to use a graded timetable, instead of starting after three years and stepping you up to being fully vested after seven years it must make you 20 percent vested after two years and 20 percent more annually after that, until you are 100 percent vested after six years.

 Top-Heavy If your company's 401(k) plan tilts towards so-called *key employees*, it is considered a *top-heavy* plan under federal law.

Your company's plan is top-heavy if key employees have more than 60 percent of all the money in your company's 401(k) plan. In other words, if you add up the value of all the accounts in your company's plan, and if the accounts owned by people who are designated key employees add up to more than 60 percent of the total, then different vesting rules apply to your company's plan. Your Plan Administrator can tell you whether your company's plan is top-heavy.

Federal law defines a key employee as any one of the following:

- A company officer earning more than half of an amount (currently $60,000) set by a federal-law formula.

- An employee who owns more than 5 percent of the company (through, for example, stock).

- An employee who owns at least 1 percent of the company and is paid at least $150,000.

- An employee who is one of the 10 largest owners of the company and whose pay exceeds an amount (currently $30,000) set by law.

The purpose of this rule is to prevent plans from benefiting higher-ranking employees more than others. A "top-heavy" situation is likely to arise in a small company that has frequent turnover of rank-and-file workers. In such a situation, federal law guarantees not only a faster vesting schedule but also that your account receives at least certain minimum contributions.

If you work for a company whose 401(k) plan is part of what is known as a *multi-employer plan*, the vesting schedule may be slower than the standard five-year and seven-year timetables described in this lesson. The schedule of your multi-employer plan will be described in the Summary Plan Description. (Multi-employer plans typically involve unionized workers for unrelated, very large corporations. Through a collective bargaining agreement, a single plan is made available to those workers even though they work for different companies.)

OTHER CONSIDERATIONS

If you're married and your spouse has a 401(k) plan at his or her work place, both of you should participate to the maximum allowable in your respective plans.

However, if you need to select one plan over the other or if you need to choose which plan to contribute more money to, decide which plan will do you the most good by retirement. You should consider such things as how much each plan allows you to contribute, which one offers better investment choices, whether both offer a company match and, if so, how much and how soon.

You should also consider which plan offers a faster vesting schedule. The sooner you can control more of the money, the better.

In this lesson, you learned what vesting is and how it works. In the next lesson you learn how to schedule contributions to your account so they cost you less.

20

BORROWING MONEY FROM YOUR ACCOUNT

In this lesson, you will learn how to borrow money from your own account, the advantages and disadvantages, and about the penalties for breaking the rules.

WHAT IS THE LOAN FEATURE AND HOW DOES IT WORK?

Like matching employer contributions and after-tax employee contributions, loans are an optional feature. Your company decides whether to allow you and other 401(k) plan participants to borrow your own money.

In fact, by a wide majority most company plans do let you borrow from your account. Similarly, plans that offer a loan feature are more popular than plans that do not.

Usually, you can use a loan from your own account for an unlimited variety of expenses, ranging from helping yourself buy a home to paying for unexpected medical bills.

However, there are myriad rules governing 401(k) plan loans. Here are 10 things you need to know about the loan feature:

1. **How can you find out whether your plan permits loans?** It cannot be arbitrary. Loans must be specifically permitted by your plan. Ask your personnel director, human resources department, or plan administrator whether loans are allowed.

2. **What are the basics of how a 401(k) plan loan works?** You borrow from your own account, and pay back the loan with interest. One key advantage is that you pay interest to your own account rather than to a bank or another commercial lender.

3. **How much can you borrow?** The limit is often described as $50,000 or half of your vested account. That is a general description of the limit. However, there are some additional regulations that shape the loan ceiling. Your loan may not be more than whichever is less:

   - $50,000, minus an amount involving all other loans from your account you have not repaid. The amount by which the $50,000 is reduced is the highest portion of your previous loan(s) that remained unpaid anytime during the preceding 12 months, even if that is more than the amount unpaid at the time you take the new loan.

   (In other words, if you borrowed $15,000 11 1/2 months earlier and only $10,000 remained unpaid when you took the second loan, the $50,000 ceiling would be reduced by the full $15,000 rather than $10,000. You would be able to borrow no more than $35,000 in the second loan.)

   Or:

   - Whichever is larger between a) $10,000 or b) 50 percent of your vested account balance.

Table 20.1 shows how to use that rule to calculate the maximum size loan you are allowed to take. If you have no loans from your account outstanding, here is how to calculate the loan-limit formula. Find where you are on the table, then follow the steps to compute your loan limit.

TABLE 20.1   YOUR LOAN LIMIT: WITH NO LOANS OUTSTANDING

IF YOUR VESTED ACCOUNT BALANCE IS:	THEN YOU MAY BORROW UP TO:
$20,000 or less	$20,000 to $100,000
More than $100,000	$10,000
50 percent of the vested amount	$50,000

If you do have at least one loan from your account outstanding, use the following steps to calculate the loan-limit formula:

Step 1.   From $50,000, subtract the highest amount you still owed at any point during the preceding 12 months on the previous loan(s).

$50,000 – X = $_____

Step 2.   Divide the vested amount in your account by 2.

(Your vested amount) ÷ 2 = $_____

Step 3.   Write the number, $10,000, in the space below:

$10,000

Step 4.   Copy whichever underlined dollar figure in steps 2 or 3 is larger:

$_____

Step 5.   Your loan limit is whichever dollar figure is smaller, the underlined one in step 1 or step 4: $_____

4. **Is there a minimum you must borrow?** Your employer may prohibit loans smaller than a certain amount of money, but the minimum may not be more than $1,000.

5. **Are there other restrictions?** One restriction is against significant business owners making loans to themselves. If you are a rank-and-file employee who owns company stock, this probably does not apply to you. But if you are a larger owner-employee of any kind, check with an appropriate person about this prohibition.

In addition, your plan may make other restrictions relating to such things as:

- The size of a loan relative to the amount you are paid.

- The number of loans you may have at any one time or in any particular period.

- Your reasons for taking a loan.

- The account or investment from which the loan is taken. This is important because it could affect your decision about taking a loan in the first place. For example, if your plan levies a loan against one of your investments, you may want to delay the loan if that investment happens to be performing particularly well at that time. Otherwise, you would be penalizing yourself by reducing how much that investment can earn.

Another option: Your plan may instead levy a loan proportionately against all of your investments.

In any case, you should also find out where the interest you pay is put. You may have choices, some of which would be more beneficial than others.

Non-Discriminatory Although your company may establish restrictions, it is not allowed to restrict loans for such reasons as race, color, religion, sex, age, or national origin.

6. **How much will it cost?** The interest rate will be about the same as interest charged by banks and other commercial lenders in your area for similar loans. Your company's plan may also charge you a service fee to process a loan.

7. **Is the interest deductible?** Generally, no.

8. **How quickly must you repay your loan?** Within five years. However, if you take a loan to buy a principal residence your plan may give you a longer period of time to repay. Loans to improve your home, buy a vacation home or any second home, or to help a family member buy a home are subject to the five-year limit.

In either case, it must be repaid through at least four quarterly installments yearly. If you don't repay the loan within five years (or if you borrow more than you're supposed to), your loan usually becomes an early "distribution" subject to income tax as well as a 10 percent penalty.

9. **Does your spouse have to consent to the loan?**
Possibly. If so, your spouse may have to give written
permission for any loan within 90 days before the
loan is supposed to be made. Ask your plan administrator if your plan requires spousal consent.

10. **Do you have to provide collateral for the
loan?** Yes, you have to give something as security
for the loan. When you offer your vested account
balance as collateral (which is what most people do),
you will not be allowed to pledge more than half of
that as collateral.

THE PROS AND CONS OF BORROWING

Before you borrow from your own account, you must decide
whether the benefits outweigh the costs.

The advantages include:

- Motivation to enroll in your company's plan.

- Access to money in a financial emergency.

- Ease of borrowing—unlike a bank loan, generally, you
aren't required to submit a financial statement or
other proof of your credit worthiness to get a loan.

The disadvantages, however, can be significant:

- When you withdraw money from your 401(k) account, you are preventing that money from growing
towards your retirement nest egg. You must decide
whether your need for a loan outweighs this loss. In
any event, you should not borrow money from your
401(k) account to pay for everyday expenses.

- If you are laid-off or unexpectedly switch jobs, instead of five years, you may have only as little as 60 days to repay your loan—without advance warning. Failure to do so can result in taxes and penalties.

- There are potential hidden costs. If you borrow by cashing in shares of a mutual fund or stock when the market is down, replacing those same shares after the market rises will cost you more money.

- You can throw your asset allocation strategy out of alignment. For example, if you borrow from a fixed-income investment, you may reduce its share of your total account or portfolio below what you want. If you do that during a period when the stock market is performing worse than the bond market, you will reduce your overall portfolio's return.

- Double taxation: Unlike regular, before-tax contributions to your account, interest payments are with after-tax dollars—that is, take-home pay on which you've paid taxes. After you retire, you will have to pay taxes on earnings from those dollars as well.

The best advice? Borrow from yourself if you must. But borrow as little and as infrequently as possible.

In this lesson, you learned how to borrow money from your own plan, when you should do so and what it will cost to borrow from yourself. In the next lesson, you will learn how to withdraw money from your account for a financial emergency.

HARDSHIP DISTRIBUTION

In this lesson, you will learn how to withdraw money from your account for financial emergencies, and what the costs are.

Another feature your company may include in its 401(k) plan is the opportunity for you to make emergency withdrawals from your account. If your company's plan includes this option, you would be allowed to make a so-called *hardship withdrawal* to pay for a serious financial emergency.

The hardship withdrawal resembles the loan feature in that both involve withdrawing money from your account before retirement, an action that federal regulations generally discourage. Furthermore, both are options included in your plan at the discretion of your company.

But important differences exist between the two.

THE KEY DIFFERENCES

- Hardship withdrawals are severely restricted, usually permitted only for specific purposes outlined by law. On the other hand, you can use a loan for almost any purpose; your company, rather than the law, is more likely to limit those uses.

- As a consequence of making a hardship withdrawal, you may be barred from contributing to your account for a year. That would deprive you of a year's worth of money growing inside your nest egg.

- A hardship withdrawal costs you money in the form of taxes and a 10 percent penalty, whereas a loan, while reducing the amount of your money that grows through compounding, earns you money in the form of interest.

- A loan has to be repaid. A hardship withdrawal does not.

Thus, a hardship withdrawal is usually more costly and difficult. Nevertheless, the chance to make a hardship withdrawal can be a financial lifesaver. It turns your 401(k) account into a friendly lender-of-last-resort.

HOW TO QUALIFY FOR A HARDSHIP WITHDRAWAL

In order to use a hardship withdrawal you must meet numerous conditions:

- You are allowed to use it only to pay for a serious, current financial emergency ("an immediate and heavy financial need," in Internal Revenue Service jargon).

- You are allowed to withdraw only enough to pay for the financial need.

- You have to use all other available sources of money from your plan, including loans, before you're allowed to make a hardship withdrawal.

- You may have to document your financial-hardship expenses and prove to your employer that you cannot get money from any other source.

Generally, you are eligible for a hardship withdrawal only for four purposes:

- To pay for certain medical expenses incurred by you, your spouse, or your dependents.

- To cover tuition and related fees for the next year of post-secondary education for you, your spouse, or your dependents.

- To purchase your principal home.

- To prevent your eviction from or foreclosure on your principal home.

Tax laws may permit your plan to allow you to make a hardship withdrawal for certain other reasons. Check with your Plan Administrator or a benefits counselor at your company.

In this lesson, you learned how to withdraw money from your account for financial emergencies. In the next lesson, you will learn about your rights and obligations in the event of certain crises.

22

COPING WITH LIFE'S EMERGENCIES

In this lesson, you will learn how to use your 401(k) account in emergencies.

You may wonder what happens to your 401(k) account when certain emergencies occur. Federal and state laws provide you with certain rights and impose certain obligations.

DIVORCE OR FAMILY SUPPORT

Generally, your retirement benefits cannot be taken away from you by people to whom you owe money. The law makes exceptions in the case of divorce or family support, however. Your spouse, former spouse, child, or other dependent may be entitled to a share of your 401(k) account. The amount will vary, according to your circumstances and state law requirements.

A state court can award some share of your account by issuing what is called a *qualified domestic relations order* (QDRO). The QDRO (pronounced quadro) must specify the amount or percentage of your account to be paid in alimony, child support, or marital property rights, (or it must specify a method for determining that amount or percentage). It also must specify the recipient and the number of payments or time period involved.

The order cannot call for a type or form of payment that your account's plan has not already offered to its participants. Nor can it order your plan to pay more than your account can afford.

Your spouse or former spouse will probably be entitled to the same rights as any plan participant. That would include leaving his or her share of your account invested in the 401(k) plan, unless the court orders it to be taken out. If your spouse withdraws his or her share, he or she will have to pay income tax on it (but not an early-withdrawal penalty), even if your spouse is older than 59 1/2 or otherwise eligible for a penalty-free withdrawal.

IN THE EVENT OF YOUR DEATH

Your spouse is automatically presumed to be your beneficiary by your 401(k) plan. If you die before you receive your benefits (payments or *distributions* from your account), all of your benefits will automatically go to your surviving spouse. Your spouse will be allowed to roll it over into an Individual Retirement Account (IRA) or withdraw the money. If your spouse withdraws the money, he or she will have to pay income taxes on it but not the early-withdrawal penalty.

If you want to select someone other than your spouse as your beneficiary, your spouse must consent in writing, witnessed by a notary or a plan representative. A non-spouse beneficiary will have fewer rights, however. For example, only your spouse is allowed to move assets from your account into a rollover IRA, protected from taxes.

When you reach a *distribution date*, such as retirement age, you may select without your spouse's consent any of the forms of payment offered by your company's plan. If a *life annuity* is one of those options and you choose it, your spouse is then protected by what are known as the *qualified joint and survivor annuity* (QJSA) rules and your plan benefits will be paid according to those rules unless you and your spouse agree to some different method of payment.

Distribution Date   A time when you become eligible to take money out of your account without a 10 percent early-withdrawal penalty. These eligibility dates are explained in Lesson 5.

QJSA Rules   A *qualified joint and survivor annuity* is one that provides a series of equal, periodic payments after you reach a distribution date like retirement to you and then to your surviving spouse. The payments to your spouse have to be at least half of what you and your spouse received while you were still alive, and the payments may not be more than 100 percent of that either. This sort of annuity is much more common in a defined-benefit or traditional pension plan.

More Information   If you want more information about QJSA rights, ask the Internal Revenue Service for a copy of IRS Publication 1565, "Looking Out for #2: A Married Couple's Guide to Understanding Your Benefit Choices at Retirement from a Defined Contribution Plan." You may call the IRS at 202-622-6074.

In any event, when you die your plan usually fully vests any of your company's matching contribution in which you were not yet 100 percent vested. That would go to your beneficiary in whatever manner you have arranged for under your plan's rules.

Your Summary Plan Description (see Lesson 4) will tell you what your plan's rules are for survivor benefits.

IF YOUR PLAN ENDS

Although your company is required to start a 401(k) plan with the intention of continuing it, circumstances may arise that cause your company to end your plan.

If that happens, you become 100 percent vested in your accrued benefits when the plan is terminated. Also, you can keep your account tax-deferred by having it transferred directly into a rollover IRA.

If your company goes out of business, you cannot lose your account to your company's creditors. Your company's plan is in what is known as a *trust* account, which is legally separate from the company. If your company goes out of business, your 401(k) plan is not part of its assets and creditors cannot claim it as repayment for your company's debts.

If your plan is terminated because your company merges with or is taken over by another business and you enroll in your new employer's plan, you will be subject to its rules even if they are less generous than your old plan's. You can keep any investments from your old plan that are not options in your new plan simply by moving them into a rollover IRA.

In this lesson, you learned about your rights and obligations in the event of various difficulties. In the next lesson, you will learn how to make sure your company is not illegally using your 401(k) account money for its own purposes.

ACKNOWLEDGMENTS

Contributions to analysis: David Wray, Profit Sharing/401(k) Council of America; Dee Lee, Harvard Financial Educators; Internal Revenue Service; U.S. Department of Labor.

23

SAFEGUARDING YOUR ACCOUNT

In this lesson, you will learn how to make sure your company is not illegally using your 401(k) account money for its own purposes.

One of the biggest differences between a traditional pension plan and your 401(k) plan is that most traditional pension plans are insured by the Pension Benefit Guaranty Corp. (PBGC), a federal agency. That means if a company's pension plan falls short of money to pay retirement benefits, the PBGC's job is to make up the difference.

Your 401(k) plan has no such insurance.

TEN WARNING SIGNS

The need for wariness was highlighted in late 1995 when the U.S. Department of Labor announced it was investigating several hundred companies (mostly small and mid-size) for possible improper use of 401(k) contributions.

Many of the targeted companies were using the money to cover business expenses. Only a handful of companies were accused of actual theft. The vast majority of the 228,000 companies conducting plans are free of fraud.

Therefore, while the federal investigation is important, you should not be overly alarmed. You shouldn't withdraw from or delay enrolling in your company's plan.

Still, you can and should take certain precautions. If you find any danger signals, ask your company's employee benefits office for an explanation. If you are not reassured by what you are told, contact the federal Pension and Welfare Benefits Administration (PWBA) at 202-219-8776 (or look for a regional office phone number in your local telephone book). Warning signs include:

- Your 401(k) account statement (which is sent to you four times a year or at other regular intervals) is consistently late or arrives at irregular intervals.

- Your account balance does not appear to be accurate. One way to check this is by comparing contributions shown on your statement to those shown on your paycheck stub; the year-to-date deductions on your paycheck should match your statement.

One Red Flag   One explanation for a discrepancy between what you have contributed (the amount that will be shown on your pay stub) and the amount that shows up on your statement is that your company may have as long as 90 days to deposit your money in your account.

If your money takes longer than 90 days to show up on your statement—or is not showing up at all—your company is handling your money improperly. At best, your company is using it as a loan from you without paying you interest.

As a result of his agency's investigation, the Secretary of Labor has proposed tighter deposit deadlines. Deadlines as short as one week or less larger companies and up to 30 days for smaller businesses may be adopted.

Your company's matching contribution, if any, is probably handled differently. Your company has up until one whole year to pay its contribution; it is allowed to make its entire year's worth of payments all at once annually.

* Your account balance drops significantly in a way that cannot be explained by normal market fluctuations.

* Former employees are having trouble getting their benefits paid on time or in correct amounts.

* Investments listed on your statement are not what you selected.

* Frequent or unexplained changes in investment managers.

* Unusual transactions or expenses, such as a loan to officers of your company or to one of the trustees of your 401(k) plan. Check your plan's annual report to spot such things.

* Your company's matching contribution does not show up on your statement. If in doubt, ask your mutual fund, insurance company (if you have insurance-related investments), benefits counselor, investment manager or plan administrator for the date and amount of recent contributions to your account.

- Your efforts to get account information go unanswered. This is more likely to be a sign of trouble if your company is a small business, which issues account statements rather than using an outside investment manager to do so.

- Your company is experiencing severe financial difficulty and cuts expenses, drops its outside payroll service, and instead starts to issue paychecks itself. That makes it difficult for you to determine whether your contributions and any company match are flowing into your account, and on time. Of course, not all companies resort to misusing their employees' money for their own financial benefit. But such circumstances warrant wariness.

Where To Start   The first place to look for information about how your plan should work is its Summary Plan Description (SPD). The SPD outlines all of your plan's procedures; explains how contributions are deposited in your account; identifies key people like the plan Trustees and the Plan Administrator and where you can reach them; and describes how your eligibility and vesting are determined.

Remember: Errors in record keeping do happen. You can minimize your chances of being victimized by fraud by keeping a calm but appropriate watch over your account.

In this lesson, you learned how to protect your 401(k) plan account from being misused by your company or some unethical officer of your company.

INDEX

A

accounts
    contributions
        options (listing of), 97-99
        restrictions, 99-101
    safeguarding, 129-131
accrued benefits, 108
after-tax contributions,
  106-107
annual distributions, 21
    recalculation method, 22
    term certain, 21
annual savings, 32-33
annuities (buying), 21
annuitized distributions, 18
annuity factors, 29-30
assets (allocation), 69-74

B

back-end load (mutual fund
  sales charges), 95
balanced funds, 67
benefits, 2-4
    accrued benefits, 108
    beneficiaries, 126-127
    death (QJSA), 127
    individual benefit state-
      ment, 14
    receiving
        distribution date, 127
        in the event of death,
        126-127
    sharing
        divorce, 125-126
        family support, 125-126
bond, 63
borrowing (from your
  account), 115-120
    loan limits, 117
business risk, 37-39
    time factors, 51-54

C

cash equivalent, 64
company restrictions
  (account contributions), 100
company rules, 82-86
    your right to plan
      information, 83-85
company stocks, 68
compounding, 44-49
contributions
    after-tax contributions,
      106-107
    matching contributions,
      102-105
        unclear incentive rates,
        104-107

options (listing of), 97-99
restrictions, 99-101
current savings status, 30

D

defined-contribution plan, 2
distribution date (death benefits), 127
distributions (annual), 21
recalculation method, 22
term certain, 21
diversification (defined), 41
options, 42
divorce (sharing benefits), 125-126

E

early withdrawal penalties (taxes), 19
eligibility
enrollment standards, 10-11
withdrawals, 17-19
employees, key employees, 113
enrollment, 10-11
entitled information, 83-85
Summary Plan Description (SPD), 83
equal credit (eligibility), 11
expenses (mutual funds), 92-96
operating expenses, 94
plan fees, 96
sales charges, 94-96

F

family support, 125-126
"fixed-income" investments, 65
fixed dollar amount to invest, 33-35

forward averaging (taxes), 21
front-end load (mutual fund sales charges), 95
funds
mutual funds
expenses, 92-96
information sources, 87
operating expenses, 94
plan fees, 96
sales charges, 94-96
stock funds
balanced funds, 67
growth and income funds, 66
growth funds, 66
international funds, 68
lifestyle funds, 68
sector funds, 67
small-company funds, 67

G

growth and income funds, 66
growth funds, 66

H

hardship withdrawals, 122-123
qualifications, 123-124
highly compensated employee (HCE), 99

I

income
Request for Earnings and Benefit Estimate Statement, 28
yearly income in retirement, 28
individual benefit statement, 14

inflation risk, 37, 39-40
information sources
    entitled information, 83-85
        Summary Plan Description (SPD), 83
    individual benefit statement, 14
    inside, 85-86
    investment manager, 13
    measuring mutual fund performance, 89-91
    outside, 86
        specializing in mutual funds, 87
    plan administrator, 13
    QJSA (IRS), 127
    recordkeeper, 13
    sponsor, 12
    summary annual report, 14
    summary of material modifications, 14
    summary plan description, 13
    trustee, 12
interest risk (defined), 37
international funds, 68
investment manager, 13
investments
    asset allocation, 69-74
    bond (defined), 63
    cash equivalent, 63-64
    compounding, 45-49
    diversification (defined), 41
        options, 42
    "fixed-income", 65
    investment manager, 13
    loans, 64-66
    market-timing (defined), 43
    mutual fund (defined), 63
    options for investing less, 35

rate of return, 26
safety (defined), 62
selecting, 75-78
    asset-allocation, 78
    avoiding new funds and managers, 77-78
    diversification, 76
    investing for growth, 76-77
    investing long term, 77
    timeliness, 76
stock funds, 66-74
    balanced funds, 67
    growth and income funds, 66
    international funds, 68
    lifestyle funds, 68
    sector funds, 67
    small-company funds, 67
stocks, 63, 66-74
IRS, 127

K-L

key employees (defined), 113

lifestyle funds, 68
loans, 64-66
    borrowing from your account, 115-120
        loan limits, 117
    cash equivalent, 64
    "fixed-income" investments, 65

M

market risk (defined), 37
market-timing (defined), 43
matching contributions, 102-105
    unclear incentive rates, 104-107

mutual funds (defined), 63
>expenses, 92-96
>>*operating expenses, 94*
>>*plan fees, 96*
>>*sales charges, 94-96*
>information sources, 87
>measuring performance
>>*information sources (listing of), 89-91*
>>*total return, 89-91*

N-O-P

national regulations, 79-81
>401(k), 80
>404(c), 81
no-load (mutual fund sales charges), 95

operating expenses, mutual funds (12b-1 fee), 94
other sources of income, 28

payments
>annuitized distributions (withdrawals), 18
>setting intervals, 21
Pension and Welfare Benefits Administration (PWBA), 130
plan administrator, 13
plans
>401(k) plans
>>*advantages, 2, 5-6*
>>*features, 2-4*
>defined-contribution plan, 2
>fees (mutual funds), 96
>plan termination, 128
prohibitions (withdrawals), 19-20
prospectus (defined), 84

Q

QJSA
>information sources (IRS), 127
>regulations (qualified joint and survivor annuity), 127
qualifications (hardship withdrawals), 123-124

R

rate of return (defined), 26
>conservative estimates, 26
recalculation method (annual distributions), 22
receiving benefits
>distribution date, 127
>in the event of death, 126-127
recordkeeper, 13
remaining savings shortfall, 32
restrictions
>account contributions, 99-101
>>*company restrictions, 100*
>>*voluntary limits, 99-100*
>highly compensated employees (HCE), 99
retirement
>annual distributions, 21
>>*recalculation method, 22*
>>*term certain, 21*
>annuities (buying), 21
>payment intervals, 21
>withdrawal options, 21
retirement savings worksheet, 28-35
>annual savings, 32-33
>annuity factors, 29-30
>closing the gap, 29-30

current savings status, 30

fixed dollar amount to invest, 33-35

gap in desired annual income, 29

other sources of income, 28

savings growth factor, 30-31

yearly income in retirement, 28

risk

business risk, 37-39

time factors, 51-54

diversification, 41

inflation risk, 37, 39-40

interest risk (defined), 37

market risk (defined), 37

risk tolerance (defined), 56

change patterns, 56-60

rules

company rules, 82-86

your right to plan information, 83-85

national regulations, 79-80

401(k), 80

404(c), 81

S

safeguarding accounts, 129-131

sales charges (mutual funds), 94-96

back-end load, 95

front-end load, 95

no-load, 95

savings

annual, 32-33

compounding, 45-49

current savings status, 30

savings growth factor, 30-31

savings shortfall, 32

sector funds, 67

selecting investments, 75-78

asset-allocation adjustments, 78

avoiding new funds and managers, 77-78

diversification, 76

investing for growth, 76-77

investing long term, 77

timeliness, 76

small-company funds, 67

sponsor, 12

stock funds, 66-74

balanced funds, 67

growth and income funds, 66

lifestyle funds, 68

international funds, 68

sector funds, 67

small-company funds, 67

stocks, 63, 66-74

company stocks, 68

summary annual report, 14

summary of material modifications, 14

summary plan description, 13

Summary Plan Description (SPD), 83-85, 132

T

telephone numbers

IRS, 127

Pension and Welfare Benefits Administration (PWBA), 130

term certain (annual distributions), 21

time factors (business risk), 51-54

top-heavy plans (vesting), 113

total return (defined), 88

mutual funds (measuring performance), 89-91

trustee (information sources), 12

U-V

unclear incentive rates (matching contributions), 104-107

vesting, 109-110
  advantages, 110-114
    additional rules, 111-114
  avoiding tax penalties, 112
  top-heavy plans, 113
voluntary limits (account contributions), 99-100

W

withdrawals, 19-22
  after leaving a job, 20
  annual distributions, 21
  annuities (buying), 21
  annuitized distributions, 18
  avoiding tax liability, 20
  early withdrawal penalties (taxes), 19
  eligibility, 17-19
  hardship withdrawals, 122-123
    qualifications, 123-124
  options when retiring, 21
  payment intervals, 21
  prohibitions, 19-20
  transferring accounts, 20

Y

yearly income in retirement
yield (defined), 89